PENGUIN BOOKS

James I

Thomas Cogswell is Professor of History at the University of California Riverside. He is the author of *The Blessed Revolution: English Politics and the Coming of War, 1621–1624*; *Home Divisions: Aristocracy, the State and Provincial Conflict* and (with Alastair Bellany) *The Murder of King James I*. He is currently writing a dual biography of the Duke of Buckingham and his assassin, Lt. John Felton.

GW00360360

THOMAS COGSWELL

James I
The Phoenix King

PENGUIN BOOKS

PENGUIN BOOKS

UK | USA | Canada | Ireland | Australia
India | New Zealand | South Africa

Penguin Books is part of the Penguin Random House group of companies
whose addresses can be found at global.penguinrandomhouse.com

First published by Allen Lane 2017
First published in Penguin Books 2019
001

Set in 9.5/13.5 pt Sabon LT Std
Typeset by Jouve (UK), Milton Keynes
Printed and bound in Great Britain by Clays Ltd, Elcograf S.p.A.

ISBN: 978-0-141-98992-1

www.greenpenguin.co.uk

Penguin Random House is committed to a
sustainable future for our business, our readers
and our planet. This book is made from Forest
Stewardship Council® certified paper.

Contents

In Memory of William Robert Cogswell (1960–2015)

Introduction

Many years ago, when I first began studying King James, I found him an unappealing, irritable old man. At the end of his reign, he stubbornly blocked any efforts to assist his daughter Elizabeth and her husband, Frederick V, then struggling to recover their lands in the Palatinate. Confused by his actions, most of his subjects did not mourn his passing early in 1625. But their opinion soon changed after his son did intervene in the Palatine war in 1625–9, with uniformly disastrous results, and their assessment of James rose higher still after Charles plunged Britain into civil war a decade later. Likewise my own opinion of the first Stuart monarch softened on better acquaintance, and this new sympathy for him informs this book.

James's flaws were readily apparent. He was overly loquacious, impulsively generous, mathematically challenged and resolutely private. Yet he was eminently quotable and often amusing, and while some suffered at his hands, most found him merciful. His religious policy was equally moderate. It is notable that only a few hundred separatists felt obliged to leave James's England, while twenty thousand Puritans later fled from his son's regime. While he lacked the martial flair of Edward III and Henry V, he did preside over the Scottish 'conquest' of England, one of the most astonishing expansions in the early modern period. Admittedly, in an era when other rulers were more aggressive, James sounded somewhat naïve by repeatedly quoting I Kings 4:25, which described how under King Solomon every man sat unafraid under his own vine and fig tree. Nevertheless his attitude was attractive, and it still is. As our age has become more tolerant, we can finally comprehend something of James's emotional life and appreciate the anguish he felt when love and affection became entangled in politics and law.

This volume's modest length presents its own problems. To cope with this, I have tried to let James tell his own story, avoiding as much as possible the remarkably vivid, and partisan, histories of him that were later written during the Civil War. Likewise I have focused as much on his personal as his public life, in the hope of presenting a more vivid portrait of this underappreciated monarch.

Note on the Text

One of the more baffling aspects of early modern history is the tendency of prominent individuals to acquire a string of new titles. To simplify the situation, I have used only their highest title. Thus Robert Cecil is not Sir Robert, Lord Cecil or Viscount Cranbourne, but simply the Earl of Salisbury. Likewise spellings and punctuation have been modernized in quotations from contemporary sources, and the New Year is assumed to have begun on 1 January, not 25 March.

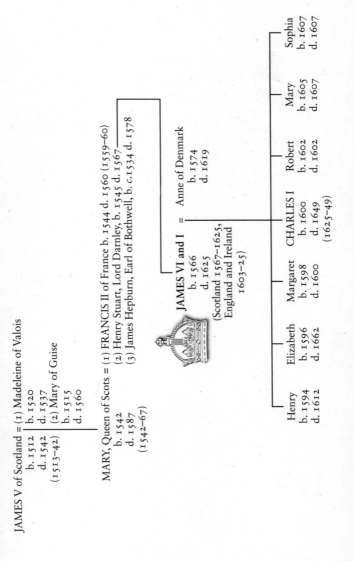

JAMES V of Scotland = (1) Madeleine of Valois
b. 1512   b. 1520
d. 1542   d. 1537
(1513–42)   (2) Mary of Guise
                 b. 1515
                 d. 1560

MARY, Queen of Scots = (1) FRANCIS II of France b. 1544 d. 1560 (1559–60)
b. 1542   (2) Henry Stuart, Lord Darnley, b. 1545 d. 1567
d. 1587   (3) James Hepburn, Earl of Bothwell, b. c.1534 d. 1578
(1542–67)

JAMES VI and I   =   Anne of Denmark
b. 1566   b. 1574
d. 1625   d. 1619
(Scotland 1567–1625,
England and Ireland
1603–25)

Henry   Elizabeth   Margaret   CHARLES I   Robert   Mary   Sophia
b. 1594   b. 1596   b. 1598   b. 1600   b. 1602   b. 1605   b. 1607
d. 1612   d. 1662   d. 1600   d. 1649   d. 1602   d. 1607   d. 1607
                                    (1625–49)

James I

Prologue
Above All the Sportsmen
in the World

In 1620, an English diplomat hurried to tell the old king about ominous continental developments. He eventually found James VI and I, not at Whitehall, but rather ambling down a country lane, surrounded by 'beagles, spaniels, greyhounds, sparrow-hawks and goshawks', looking like 'a Grand Cazador', a great huntsman. This seems improbable since we now tend to think of King James as a well-turned-out courtier, perhaps presiding at a grand occasion in the Whitehall Banqueting House. Yet he was indeed a 'Grand Cazador', someone a Venetian diplomat judged to be 'above all the sportsmen in the world'.[1]

His body revealed much about him. 'Hot, choleric and very fiery', his face was ruddy, a condition his fondness for drink only exacerbated.[2] Gout, arthritis and kidney stones troubled him, but his most distinctive feature was his slightly misshapen legs. Because they made movement difficult, he often walked leaning on others. There was nothing wrong with his lungs, however, as numerous councillors and Parliament-men could have testified. While his predecessor Elizabeth's speeches could be measured in minutes, his often ran for hours.

His volubility stemmed from his erudition, which few other rulers could have matched. Educated by George Buchanan, a celebrated Scottish scholar, James was fluent in Latin and French and could read Greek, Italian and Spanish. He displayed his talents in poetry and prose, discussing everything from tyrants to tobacco. Committed to lifelong learning, the king read widely, especially in theology, and during meals and before bed he had learned works read aloud. This background informed his style of governance. Few contemporary rulers were more adroit, and as a young man he had mastered the art of out-manoeuvring his opponents with patience and subtlety, a skill he regularly displayed during his long reign.

His pastimes were limited. Given the deformity in his legs, dancing was out of the question. Since his disability disappeared in the saddle, James was devoted to riding, and he liked cards and the occasional play. Otherwise he only had one avocation.

Hunting, which had occupied Elizabeth for a few days a year, annually consumed months of James's life. He was not choosy about quarry, pursuing otters in millstreams and hares in foul weather. Deer, however, were his favourite. He kept the herds in his hunting parks well stocked and well fed. Anxious to preserve their numbers, James energetically pursued not only poachers but also presumptuous officials who helped themselves to his deer, and moles whose burrows might injure them.

Although some depicted him as cowardly, the deer would have told a different story. The king was merciful, a contemporary remarked, 'except at the chase, where he was cruel'. Rather than shoot the animals as they ran past – Elizabeth I's method – James liked to chase a stag for miles with his dogs, and once he brought one down, he would cut it open, 'put his arm entirely into the belly and entrails of the beast', feed the viscera to his hounds and daub his companions' faces with blood. While age slowed him, he could not resist 'to come in at the death of the deer, and to hear the commendations of his hounds'. Indeed, he confessed to dreaming about the chase.[3]

This practice had obvious dangers. Falls were common, and kidnapping or even assassination possible. Yet James would not stop. Some thought his behaviour selfish; in 1623 a man exclaimed in an alehouse: 'I would that his deer were hanged and he too.' In response, James insisted that hunting did not prevent him from attending to business. He always kept a secretary by his side, and, besides, 'he could do as much business in one hour as others would in a day.' He also added a medical excuse: 'he would die if he gave up exercise.' His doctors agreed: 'constant exercise is his salvation.'[4]

He loved country life. Admittedly he sometimes donned elegant clothes and jewels, as he regularly did on St George's Day when he paraded with the other Garter knights. Yet he was more often in ordinary, and often soiled, clothes. His dislike of 'pomp and gravity' in general and Whitehall Palace in particular reflected his personality. As Bishop Goodman recalled, 'he had no power to deny a man that was an importunate suitor', and this generosity was a serious issue for a ruler with towering debts. Furthermore, while Elizabeth could work a crowd, he frowned at them because 'he did not love to be looked on'.[5] It was far pleasanter to leave the city and to ride with a few friends looking for game.

Animals obsessed him. Fond of exotica, he kept lions, tigers and even an elephant to show his guests. His favourite the Duke of Buckingham knew how to get his attention; he once wrote to him about nursing a wounded bird. Packs of dogs constantly surrounded him, and he doted on a series of beloved canines – Jewel, then Irwell and finally Swalley. Not surprisingly, when presented with a copy of John Caius's book on the antiquity of Cambridge University, he replied that he had rather have had Caius's book on dogs.

His preferred locale was a hunting lodge. A diplomat explained that 'he prefers living in the country and dislikes too large a following'. Above all, he was fond of Newmarket and Royston, two hunting lodges so primitive that his wife, Queen Anne, would only rarely bring herself to visit them. But there James was happy. An envoy once found him in 'narrow, one might say, poor quarters', but the king was exultant 'in the midst of his beloved forests, full of great herds of stags and deer, hunting with enthusiasm'.[6]

This bucolic existence had a darker side. His doctors complained about his prodigious consumption of beer, wine and spirits. Drink sometimes led to scandal – once the tipsy monarch reportedly baptized a pig – and it encouraged his cruder tastes. He was renowned for deadpan humour – and bawdy language. 'King James,' Sir Robert Moray recalled, 'loved best of any discourse to talk of dirt and turds.'[7] Plainly such scandalous talk was best confined to hunting lodges. Yet profanity was the least of James's potential embarrassments.

James's 'hunting crew' consisted of a few dozen men, who also excelled at performing 'bawdy songs' and 'antic dances'. One poem captures James in this all-male environment where 'at Royston and Newmarket he will hunt until he be lean' and in the evenings 'his Jovial boys of the Rout' would 'dance a heat till they stink of sweat' and sing 'scurrilous and base stuff'.[8] In this boisterous company, his eye was often fixed on a particular man.

Handsome young men attracted him, and his emotional life had long revolved around them. The precise nature of their sexual relationship remains unclear. James adopted the role of the older, wiser man, educating surrogate sons. Yet he publicly caressed and slept with them. His sexual tastes puzzled some contemporaries and horrified others, who whispered about sodomy. These whispers cast a dark pall over James's Arcadian life. His long stays in isolated houses, a contemporary recalled, 'pleased the king's humour well, rather that he might enjoy his favourite with more privacy, then that he loved the sports'.[9]

Hunting, books, dogs and favourites all defined King James at the end of his life. But how had he developed these tastes, and how had they influenced him?

I
A Boy with a Sparrowhawk

The fashionable cap with flamboyant feathers and the pinched waist above wide flared hose first attract the viewer's attention. But details like the tight lips, the long sword and the sparrowhawk on the wrist begin to reveal the sitter's personality. The raptor is idly looking to the side, but the alert eyes of the eight-year-old James VI of Scotland never leave the viewer. (See picture 1 in the plate section.)

* * *

Mid-sixteenth-century Scotland was no country for young monarchs. Truth be told, it was not much better for the adult ones either. It was hard to govern a country with a rugged topography that made travel difficult and with unruly nobles locked in blood feuds. Aristocratic rivalries accounted for the violent deaths of no less than the Lord Chancellor Glamis in 1578 as well as the Earl of Lennox in 1571, the Earl of Eglinton in 1586, Lord Maxwell in 1593, the Earl of Arran in 1595 and two successive earls of Moray, the first in 1570 and the second in 1592. Witches reportedly killed the Earl of Angus, and poisoning allegedly claimed the Earl of Sutherland in 1567 and the Earl of Atholl in 1579. Admittedly some questioned these poisoning charges, but after Atholl's physician sought to disprove it, by licking the insides of the earl's stomach, he nearly died himself. Not even foreign guests were safe, and in 1585 Lord Russell, the son of the English Earl of Bedford, was shot during a truce on the Anglo-Scottish border.

The factionalized state reflected the bitter divisions that followed the Reformation and the emergence of the Kirk, the national reformed Church. Calvinism quickly took root in the Lowland towns, where ministers boldly rebuked monarchs as well as other wayward members of their congregation. Catholicism, however, survived among the nobility and in the Highlands. The religious turmoil in turn brought on military interventions first from the French and then from the English, and later in the century the Spanish seemed intent on invasion.

These pressures made politics within the royal household something of a contact sport. In 1566, Queen Mary, then pregnant with her son, had to watch a favourite servant being stabbed to death. Her husband Lord Darnley met an equally grim fate the following year when he was blown up in a massive explosion. Because Mary soon married the Earl of Bothwell, who was widely suspected of engineering Darnley's murder, the wedding prompted Calvinist and Catholic nobles to unite, imprisoning Queen Mary as a possible co-conspirator. With John Knox, the leading Presbyterian minister, proclaiming her a Jezebel worthy of execution, Mary was fortunate to escape to England in 1568. Tragically for her, she had to leave behind her baby.[1]

Repeated traumas punctuated her son's childhood. Because the Scottish Parliament held that Mary had abdicated, James was crowned as King of Scotland when he was thirteen months old. The infant was placed in the care of the Earl and Countess of Mar in Stirling Castle, one of the most secure locations in the realm. Mar and his kinsmen became James's surrogate family. James called Countess Arabella 'Lady Minny', Minny being a Scots name for 'mother', and she held him at his coronation.[2] The earl's younger brother Sir Alexander Erskine, the Master of Mar, was responsible for his security; and the king was raised with the Erskine boys.

The thick walls of Stirling Castle brought only intermittent peace to the young boy because his mother's supporters repeatedly tried to capture him. In 1570, one of them assassinated James's first regent, his uncle the 1st Earl of Moray. In 1571, Moray's successor, Darnley's father the Earl of Lennox, was seriously wounded during another Marian assault on Stirling. James watched his bleeding grandfather being carried into the castle, where he soon died. The next regent, the Earl of Mar himself, did not survive long. In 1572, he became violently ill after a banquet given by the Earl of Morton, who quickly replaced him as regent.

Amid the turmoil, James attended to his studies, directed by George Buchanan. The Calvinist scholar was an odd choice for this assignment because he loathed James's mother and proved ambivalent about her son. Nevertheless Buchanan drilled the young boy in history, languages and theology so relentlessly that James later quipped that he spoke Latin before he said a word of Scots. The king proved an apt pupil, and, at eight, he was the 'sweetest sight in Europe' – a young prince with 'extraordinary gifts of ingenuity, judgment, memory and language', able to recite long biblical passages and translate Latin and French.[3]

Reluctantly, Buchanan conceded that the boy needed some physical activity if only to tire him. His attendants taught him the rudiments of dance, archery and golf, and they trained him to ride a horse, a revelation for a hobbled young man. Buchanan tried to limit any hunting to a most frustrating quarry – rabbits. Yet as James's early portrait reveals, he also was already fond of hawking, a sport his grandmother the Countess of Lennox had encouraged with her gift to him of a decorated hawking glove.

Buchanan also was responsible for less pleasant aspects of James's education. In a 1571 book, he denigrated Mary and her marriage to Bothwell, 'wherein all Laws of Gods and man are violated, despised, and in a manner wholly extinguished'. Not surprisingly, he treated her son harshly. When told to control his temper, the volatile boy pointed out that lions, not lambs, were on the King of Scotland's coat of arms. Plainly he needed discipline, which Buchanan happily administered. Once when the Countess of Mar objected to him beating the boy, Buchanan replied: 'I have whipped his arse, you can kiss it if you like.' Likewise when Buchanan again beat James, this time for inadvertently killing a sparrow, he alluded to James's mother by calling the young king 'a true bird of that bloody nest'. Understandably James later had profoundly ambivalent views about his tutor. In 1618, when a bold Scots scholar publicly mocked Buchanan's faulty Latin, James, far from being upset, appointed him to a lucrative post.[4]

James received a prince's education, and at the age of eleven he had to put it into practice. In March 1578, after nearly six years of Regent Morton's rule, James VI announced that he would take over the government. Although Morton graciously retired, his supporters attempted to seize Stirling Castle. In the affray, Alexander Erskine, the Master of Mar, had to use a halberd to defend the king, and Erskine's eldest son was killed. For his part James was 'in great fear of the tumult' and anxious about his loyal servant, he 'tore his hair, saying the Master is slain'. The memory of the affray understandably 'greatly disquieted' his sleep. With civil war imminent, James's supporters marched under a plaintive banner depicting a child behind a grate and bearing two mottoes: 'Liberty I crave and cannot it have' and 'Either you shall have it or we will die for it'.[5] Later in 1578, James announced that he had come of age. Three thousand men on horseback escorted the twelve-year-old to Edinburgh, where the town presented various tableaux. One depicting Solomon made perfect sense, but another – Bacchus distributing free wine – may have been less well chosen given his later habits. The heady optimism of his entry, however, did not last.

'I was alone,' James later lamented, 'without father or mother, brother or sister.'[6] But he did have cousins, and a distant one appeared in 1579. Although Esmé Stuart, Sieur d'Aubigny, had been raised in France, he was Regent Lennox's nephew, and James was delighted when he came to visit. Finding him an ideal prop to lean on, the hobbled king kept Lennox constantly in attendance, creating him first Earl, and then Duke, of Lennox. In contrast to the more rough-hewn local style, the Frenchman brought with him the politesse of Fontainebleau, and this beau idéal encouraged the king to write poetry. Lennox also established himself as de facto regent, first arresting and then beheading Morton in 1581.

Lennox was unpopular. Calvinist ministers were deeply suspicious of him even after he abandoned the Catholic Church; Queen Elizabeth feared he would revive the Franco-Scottish 'Auld Alliance'; and most Scottish nobles resented his power with the king. They all found him a corrupting influence. He 'frequently abused' James's 'chaste ears' with 'unknown Italian and French forms of oaths, the mistress of all bawdry and villainy', and he introduced 'prodigality and vanity of apparel, superfluity in banqueting and delicate cheer, deflowering of dames and virgins and other fruits of the French court'. They even whispered that Lennox had introduced James to sodomy. Above all else, these critics feared that Lennox would bring back Queen Mary, anxieties that explain the vehement reaction to the Duke of Guise's gift of six horses in 1581. James's favourite preacher implored the king, not only to reject gifts from such a notorious papist, but also to resist Lennox's sexual temptation. The teenager smoothly responded that 'his body was clean and unpolluted'. He kept the horses.[7]

To break Lennox's power, the duke's opponents organized a coup d'état, which James's fondness for hunting

made easy. After urging the king to hunt deer near Ruthven Castle, the Earl of Gowrie and other 'Lords
Enterprisers' detained him here on 23 August 1582, and
when James began crying, one of his captors roughly responded: 'better that bairns should weep than bearded
men.'[8] They would keep him confined for nearly a year,
and after the Kirk endorsed their action, the lords ordered
Lennox out of the country. He died shortly afterwards in
France and left his embalmed heart to James.

His seizure, James later explained, was 'not good, hon-
ourable nor safe', but it was instructive. One bleak night,
he wrote on a wall 'A prisoner I am / and liberty would
have', and the next morning he found a chilling response:
'A papist you are, and friend to a slave / A rope you deserve,
and that you shall have.' The crisis transformed James.
Earlier he had written of the need 'to invent / The way to
get your own intent'. If he remembered 'Thought unre-
vealed can do no ill', then it followed that 'with patience
then see thou attend / and hope to vanquish at the end'.
This advice guided his later career. Consequently he co-
operated with his captors, and hunting, which had
ensnared him, eventually allowed his escape. After assuring his captors of his support, James 'desired that they
would grant him liberty of hunting', and in June 1583 he
finally escaped – hunting as he went.[9]

Once free, James revealed his fury: 'there was no king in
Europe would have suffered the things that he hath suffered.' His wrath was focused on the Lords Enterprisers
and on the Presbyterian ministers, all of whom were 'but a
pack of knaves', and he vowed that 'he had rather lose his

kingdom, ere he were not avenged upon them'. Although he talked about reigning as 'an universal King', a ruler 'indifferent to all our nobility and good subjects, and not to be led . . . by particular men', he soon reverted to old habits.[10]

Shortly before his escape, he learned that Lennox had died. To honour his mentor, he raised his children in Scotland, and in 1584 he printed *The Essays of a Prentice*, highlighting a poem, 'A Phoenix', describing how ignorance and jealousy had ultimately destroyed such an exotic foreign creature as Lennox. He also took Lennox's younger associate, the Earl of Arran, as his protégé. Together the two men banished the Lords Enterprisers and executed Gowrie after he botched another coup attempt. More dramatically, to check the Kirk's power, they persuaded Parliament to pass the 'Black Acts' dissolving presbyteries and proclaiming James's authority over the Church. In short order, several leading ministers joined the banished lords, then congregating in exile just across the English border in Berwick. James also took the occasion to display his family loyalty by calling in all copies of Buchanan's historical works, which were to 'the dishonour and prejudice of his highness's parents'.[11]

Having reasserted his authority, James quickly lost it. He hoped improved Anglo-Scottish relations would stabilize his position in Scotland, but in 1585 one of Arran's men killed Lord Russell on the Borders. After punishing English retaliatory raids, James had Arran arrested, but in November 1585 the banished lords invaded and captured the king. Bereft of options, James had to agree to their demands, while Arran withdrew from politics.

By this point, after two of his favourites had been driven from him, the young king seemed hopelessly inept. Yet at this bleak moment James did the unexpected. He changed.

2
The Hat with the Jewelled 'A'

The apparel is unquestionably lavish – the jacket with golden panels and buttons, and the fur-lined cloak – but the viewer's gaze is immediately drawn to the hat with the gold hatband supporting an enormous jewelled letter 'A'. By 1595, when this picture of the king was painted, James had plainly matured, as his fixed jaw and confident visage reveal. More importantly, as his hat jewel unmistakably proclaims, he had acquired a wife – Anne. (See picture 2.)

* * *

In 1584, a Frenchman who went to have an audience with James soon found himself atop a horse. The king, he discovered, 'likes hunting above all the pleasures of the world, remaining there at least six hours together chasing all over the place with loosened rein'. Because he found the teenage monarch to be unusually serious, he dubbed him 'a young old man'.[1] He would have been less surprised had he known more about James's childhood.

In 1585 after a string of older men – regents Moray, Lennox, Mar and Morton, the Duke of Lennox, the Lords Enterprisers and the Earl of Arran – had dominated his administration, James took charge using several officials, most notably the new Lord Chancellor, John Maitland of Thirlestane, to tighten his grip on the realm. He outlawed blood feuds, reconciled sparring nobles and organized processions in which former rivals paraded through the capital hand in hand. This worked as effectively as it did because James revealed that he did not nurse grudges. Thus many involved in his kidnapping in 1582 and 1585 became senior figures in his administration. James was also talented in balancing rivals against one another, and to counteract the Kirk, he tolerated a group of Catholic nobles, periodically adjusting his position towards one or the other group. In the process he made concessions to the Kirk, culminating in the 1592 Golden Act, by which the Black Acts were reversed and the presbyteries reinstated.[2]

To neutralize English interference, he signed a treaty with Elizabeth I in 1586. The agreement brought the realm peace – and James a pension of £4,000. More importantly, Elizabeth agreed not to hinder James's claim to her throne. To seal the deal, James requested a present; predictably he wanted deer. He met the shipment at Musselburgh and personally escorted them to his hunting park at Falkland Palace.[3]

Shortly after the Anglo-Scottish treaty had been signed, Queen Mary was found plotting to assassinate Elizabeth. As pressure mounted to execute her, James tried to help the mother he had not seen in twenty years. Notwithstanding Buchanan's litany of his mother's sins, he had periodically written to her, promising her in 1585 'all the contentment that a good mother can hope for from a very humble and obedient son'. To Elizabeth, he pleaded: 'my religion ever moved me to hate her course,' but 'my honour constrains me to insist for her life.' He could not save her. His most evocative response to this tragedy came in St Giles's Church in the middle of Edinburgh when James personally removed a minister from the pulpit for refusing to preach, as James had ordered, against the English treatment of Queen Mary. Following 'a murmuring and noise' from the congregation, he eventually apologized, certain that 'none of his subjects would blame him for his affections which he carried to his mother'.[4] James never could bear to hear details of her execution.

At this point, the man was beginning to emerge. He was unprepossessing; an English agent noted in 1588 that he was careless about his clothes. He regularly attended church, but he had other priorities, which an English envoy discovered when he went to worship with the king. Since James was absent, the agent concluded that 'for all the King's great professing of religion, he loves hunting better'. He was so generous that he often could not support his own household. What he really valued, an Englishman observed, was that 'he may enjoy his pleasure in hunting'. Yet, as Lord Colville noted in 1586, while James's 'great delight' was hunting, his 'private delight' was poetry, and 'in one or both of these he commonly spends the day when he has no public thing to do'. In 1587, he was thrilled when Guillaume Du Bartas, a Huguenot poet whom James greatly admired, came to visit to him, and in 1594 he issued his second book, *Poetical Exercises at Vacant Hours*.[5]

His personal foibles were also becoming apparent. His

language had coarsened. In 1592, Helen Guthrie, a woman from Aberdeen, came to see James about an urgent matter. Having found him characteristically on the way to a kennel, she reported that the vice of 'swearing' and 'filthy speaking' was widespread across the country. In response, James first laughed so hard 'that he could scarce stand on his feet'. Then he 'swore horribly'. His taste for alcohol also became noticeable. In a poem, he described how he wrote 'with pen and drink' and ended by exclaiming: 'such pith [substance] had Bacchus over me, God of wine.' Colville also noted James's 'desire to withdraw himself from places of most access and company to places of more solitude', staying there 'with very small retinue' even though it 'may endanger his person'. His tiny retinue was almost exclusively male. In 1584, a French diplomat reported that James 'loves indiscreetly', and four years later an English agent observed that the king was 'too much carried by young men that lie in his chamber'. These whispers were so insistent in 1592 that James startled the Edinburgh ministers by ordering them to preach against the common libel that he was a 'buggerer'.[6]

This extraordinary request highlighted concerns about his sexuality, concerns that would have become even more widespread if he had not married Anne of Denmark. By all accounts, he was smitten even before he had seen her. He penned amorous sonnets, and when storms delayed her arrival in 1589, he sailed to Denmark to fetch her. There he inspected Tycho Brahe's observatory, lectured Danish clerics for three hours in Latin, and – even more astonishingly – kept pace with his hosts, who were themselves renowned for their alcohol consumption. The new couple then travelled to Edinburgh, Anne in a coach and James on horseback.[7]

Sadly their relationship soon soured and from amorous verse James quickly turned to composing his 'Satire against Women', whom he described as vain, talkative and foolish. Yet notwithstanding several poems from the early 1590s, addressed to 'his Mistress', Lady Murray, James and Anne produced a series of children. On the birth of his first son, Henry, in 1594, James organized a reprise of his own infancy. He installed the young prince in Stirling Castle in the care of the aged Countess of Mar.[8] His wife protested, but he insisted. Scotland remained too unstable.

James's position had long been precarious. In 1589, he had lamented having 'the most confused state and government that ever was in any country', and in 1594 he complained of 'being utterly wearied and ashamed of the misgovernment of the country for lack of concurrence of noblemen'. An English agent noted that since the king 'is not able to command his subjects by force', his nobles 'fear him not' and James 'fears to deal with them, at least with many of them at once'.[9] As he played one against the other, James's balancing act depended on some Catholic lords. Unfortunately for him, they were often infuriating.

In 1589, the Earls of Huntly, Bothwell, Errol and Crawford rebelled in the North, and only when James marched north with his own troops did they surrender. Their behaviour became much more threatening in 1590–91 when witches purportedly confessed to plotting with Bothwell against the king's life. Bothwell, the nephew of Queen

Mary's last husband, denied all charges, but James personally interrogated the suspects. In one case, he even condemned someone who had earlier been found innocent. Subsequently, James brooded over this affair in which many were tortured and some executed, and in 1597 he produced his *Demonology* describing 'the fearful abounding at this time in this country of these detestable slaves of the Devil'.[10]

Satan soon took the form of Bothwell, who in December 1591 attacked Holyrood Palace. Although the citizens of Edinburgh eventually rescued James and Anne, John Shaw, a royal servant, died defending them. A few weeks later, amid reports of a Spanish invasion, the Catholic Huntly murdered the Protestant Earl of Moray, and an anonymous letter warned James of plots to give him 'King Richard the Second his courtesy' – that is, to depose and execute him.[11] In June 1593, Bothwell tried again, this time at Falkland Palace, driving James and Anne to hide in a tower until they were rescued. In July, Bothwell finally forced his way into James's presence. An awkward reconciliation ensued, which lasted until April 1594, when the forces of the two men clashed outside Edinburgh. The Earls of Huntly, Angus and Errol then joined Bothwell, obliging James to head north with another army, and after Bothwell fled the country, the others finally submitted. Consequently, it was more than nostalgia that prompted James to send his infant son to Stirling Castle.

After quelling the Catholic earls, James had to confront his other longstanding problem. Buchanan began his theological education, but it was the Kirk that finished it with regular criticism of his life and administration. In addition to James's alleged moral failings, the dispute between the king and the ministers centred on the Calvinist view that the monarch was subject to the Kirk, and Buchanan had even insisted that obstinate rulers could be deposed. Not surprisingly James loathed the idea of ceding such authority to the Kirk. Yet although he had abolished the presbyteries in 1584, he had been forced to allow their return in 1592. His chance to even the score came in late 1596 when religious riots erupted in Edinburgh and when some preachers attacked Queen Elizabeth as well as James himself, whom Andrew Melville, a leading minister, denigrated as no more than 'God's silly vassal'.[12]

James had been preparing for this showdown for well over a decade, developing an impressive set of responses to audacious ministers. Since most population centres were within easy reach of the capital, he could readily summon the ministers to explain themselves. Sometimes he met them in state and sometimes more casually, but invariably he used a combination of 'fear and flattery'. Livid with rage, the king would deliver a lengthy dose of 'rough countenance and speech' before trying to cajole them. The preachers quickly learned that he could trade biblical quotations with them almost indefinitely. It was equally pointless to cite the standard Presbyterian authorities. James denounced John Calvin's *Institutes of the Christian Religion* as 'childish', dismissed John Knox as 'a knave' who had called 'his mother a whore' and informed the minister who claimed a divine warrant to preach that 'the office of prophets was ended'. The preachers could only suffer his sarcasm in silence. He dubbed the godly women of Edinburgh the 'holy sisters'; and he ridiculed headstrong preachers, calling one 'a beast' and telling another: 'I will not give a turd for thy preaching!' Predictably his dogs were sometimes involved in the proceedings. Once, after berating an errant minister, he turned to a favourite hound, saying: 'I give thee more credence.'[13] Consequently, when the crisis erupted late in 1596, these earlier confrontations had left James thoroughly prepared not only to restore his authority but to expand it.

First, James did the unthinkable: he cancelled a planned hunting party. Instead he hauled preachers before him, individually and collectively, and, in one case, he even appeared unannounced at a minister's house. When one preacher grandly announced that he had a commission from God, James observed 'that is witch-like spoken', and he berated another leading Calvinist as 'a very stark fool, a heretic, an Anabaptist, a traitor to him, to the common weal, to Christ and his Kirk'. After he announced that those who would not conform to his will would lose their stipends and pensions, most grumbled but eventually complied. 'Protest if you will,' he told them, 'I will have it done.' After sending a few intransigents such as Melville into exile, James began zealously attending General Assemblies of the Kirk, which (albeit reluctantly) authorized bishops to preside over the synods and presbyteries.[14] Never before had James focused so completely on a problem, and this triumph was the crowning achievement of his reign in either kingdom.

His writing in this period reflected these struggles. In 1598, he published *The True Law of Free Monarchies* to correct the 'many endless calamities, miseries and confusions' of 'our so long disordered, and distracted Commonwealth'. Arguing against both radical Calvinists in Scotland and the Catholic League in France, he reiterated that any rebellion was unlawful because 'Kings are called Gods' and 'sit upon God his Throne in the earth'. The following year he returned to this theme in *Basilikon Doron*, his best-selling book of advice to his son. His Scottish subjects knew precisely who he meant when he attacked 'brain-sick and heady Preachers' who, having 'got such a guiding of the people', began 'to fantasize to themselves a Democratic form of government' and then deposed rulers like James's mother. For him, bishops were vital in his struggle against 'rash-heady Preachers, that think it their honour to contend with Kings, and perturb whole Kingdoms'.[15] By the time these works came out, they were effectively marking his victory over the Kirk.

By 1600, James had achieved a formidable position. He had two sons and a daughter, a national Church increasingly under his control, and nobles more peaceful than they had ever been. Yet there still were nasty surprises. On 5 August 1600, again while hunting, James was lured to Gowrie Castle, and the ensuing event – probably another botched kidnapping – left the Earl of Gowrie and his brother dead and James terrified. The king annually celebrated his deliverance, although many contemporaries were mystified about what had actually taken place.[16]

Notwithstanding this alarming incident, James VI had become an impressive ruler. He did not pursue hopeless vendettas, and when placed in a difficult position, he

instinctively played for time while he restlessly man-
oeuvred, trying to divide his enemies. To be sure, this sensible
strategy was inglorious. Yet while it would not bring him
immediate acclaim, it might eventually allow him to divide
his enemies and to bring them to terms. In the meantime,
James could always find solace in the countryside. Above
all else, he had learned to be patient. This policy had served
him well in 1582–3 while the Lords Enterprisers held him
captive and again in the early 1590s with Bothwell's
repeated rebellions. Patience, however, brought its richest
reward in March 1603, when he rejoiced that his great-
grandmother had been Henry VIII's sister.

His relationship with Queen Elizabeth was unequal and
at times demeaning. He respectfully called her 'sister' and
occasionally 'mother', Elizabeth being his godmother. For
her part, while she could be charming, she was more often
gruff. Yet notwithstanding her repeated slights, James
rarely objected. When, for example, she disparaged James's
'diseased state' and his 'careless government', when she
predicted that, unless he followed her advice, he would
'never possess [his] dignity long', when she marvelled that
James would 'tolerate so oft, so dangerous and oppro-
brious contempts', when she termed him 'a seduced king',
misled by his councillors, when she urged him to behave in
a 'kingly' manner, when she wondered why he would
'throw [him]self into the whirlpool of bottomless dis-
credit', he made no serious effort to defend himself and his
policies. Instead he meekly replied, as he had in 1601, that
he would not 'suffer any misconstrued thoughts against
any of your actions to take harbour in my heart'.[17]

His forbearance seemed almost superhuman. But on 26 March 1603, he had a very rich reward. Late that evening, Robert Carey, an English courtier, weary after a punishing three-day gallop from London, pounded on the gate at Holyrood Palace and awoke the king. He delivered the blue sapphire ring that James had earlier sent to Lady Scrope, one of the queen's attendants, for her to send on Elizabeth's death. Carey then was the first person to greet James as King of England.

3
The Mirror of Great Britain

John de Critz's 1604 portrait of James depicts a confident man whose gloves, rapier and hat all testify that he had made it. The elaborate collar and the great George insignia of the Order of the Garter identify him as James VI and I, and the enormous jewel in his hat – the 'Mirror of Great Britain' – announces his greatest ambition. (See picture 3.) Unfortunately for him, James quickly became distracted because, as he later confessed to Parliament, he thought every day in England was Christmas. It took him several years before he appreciated the error of this assumption. But first he enjoyed himself.

*　*　*

The Tudors had been re-engineering the realm for a century. Aristocratic rivalries that made sixteenth-century Scotland so turbulent certainly existed in England, but after the bloodletting of the Wars of the Roses, these quarrels were conducted in lawsuits and electoral contests. Not surprisingly, in 1601 when the Earl of Essex tried to force his way into Elizabeth's presence, a practice all too common – and sometimes successful – in Scotland, he was quickly arrested. Again in contrast with the fates of those who tried the same manoeuvre north of the Tweed, Elizabeth did not let Essex escape with his life. English rulers also had much more money than their Scottish counterparts, a fact that made it much easier for James I to secure large loans, and he had more patronage to dispense.

Initially Carey's announcement had seemed too good to be true. It did not really sink in until James's representative brought him the keys to the great English fortress at Berwick and congratulatory messages began pouring in. After an emotional farewell to the people of Edinburgh, he rode south.

Fresh wonders constantly greeted him. Every day the crowds grew larger, the shouts of 'God save King James' louder, and the gifts more lavish. Exultant, James showed off his equestrian skills, once galloping thirty-seven miles in less then four hours. He was trying to hurry, but he had not even made it to Newcastle before he was transfixed by what he saw outside Widdrington Castle. Having spotted a large herd of deer, he paused long enough to slaughter two bucks.

The next few weeks were a blur. Scarlet-clad magistrates, cheering people and stunning entertainments – at York, wine ran in specially designed troughs – all soon became a little surreal. In Lincolnshire, a hundred men on stilts greeted him, and at Godmanchester seventy teams of horses and ploughs lined up for inspection. Along the way, James helped himself to the game, and word of the new king's passion ran ahead of him. At Worksop, the huntsmen invited him to inspect the deer; outside Stamford the inhabitants had rounded up rabbits for him to hunt; and in

Cambridgeshire Sir Oliver Cromwell gave him horses, hounds and hawks. Well might he later term his ride to London as 'a hunting journey'.[1]

In Hertfordshire, the Secretary of State, Robert Cecil, welcomed him to Theobalds House, which James adored; the residence soon came into his hands. The cacophony only grew louder as James entered London itself, where 'the shouts and clamours were so great that one could scarce hear another speak'.[2]

James rose to the occasion. He smoothly replied to Latin orations, and he revealed his dry wit. After Lord Lumley boasted about his ancestors, James quipped: 'I did na ken Adam's name was Lumley.'[3] In York, he exhibited his sense of justice; when the mayor and the Lord President of the Council of the North squabbled over which of them should bear the sword before the king, James intervened, giving the honour to the Earl of Cumberland, an old warrior who actually knew how to handle a weapon. His liberality delighted contemporaries. He tipped the landlord at the Bear in Doncaster with a valuable royal lease; he knighted no fewer than 906 men; and he showered peerages on Elizabeth's administrative elite.

While he planned to unify both countries, he first set up two administrations. In Scotland, he left the Privy Council, dominated by the Earl of Dunfermline and his old childhood friend the Earl of Mar. In Westminster, he retained almost all of Elizabeth's senior officers and added some Scottish friends, most notably the Duke of Lennox, the Earl of Dunbar and the Master of Mar's son, the Earl of Kellie. Lennox eventually became the Lord Steward, and Dunbar the Chancellor of the Exchequer. In a reprise of his father's role at Stirling, Kellie was made Captain of the Guard. Along with them came many other Scotsmen, who almost completely dominated his bedchamber staff. In short order the Exchequer was paying these men and their friends back in Scotland annual pensions totalling roughly £12,000.

His English ministers tried to bring James back down to earth with sobering financial news. The state had an annual ordinary income of roughly £325,000 – and a debt of £400,000. The country was also at war with Spain, and Ireland was in revolt. Even with parliamentary subsidies, which brought in another £140,000, expenses greatly exceeded income, and the subsidies would end in 1604. To his credit, James took immediate action. Although often depicted as a coward, he more properly was intensely pragmatic. In Scotland, he had led military expeditions against rebellious nobles, but he knew that with limited resources it was wiser to play the peacemaker. Convinced that the war had exhausted England, he made peace with Spain. With the Irish rebels, he adopted the practical policy he had perfected in Scotland: he pardoned their offences, provided they accepted his authority.[4]

Having relieved these external crises, James created an internal one as household expenditures quickly doubled and then tripled those of Elizabeth. Neither he nor his wife, for example, could resist jewellery, which consumed some £130,000 in James's first six years in England, roughly a third of the crown's annual income. Unable to stop the 'mindless and unseasonable profusion of expenses', he acknowledged that 'it is a horror to me to think upon the height of my honour, the greatness of my debts and the smallness of my means'. In his defence, maintaining Elizabeth's frugality was impossible for a ruler with a wife and children, and austerity was inadvisable for a foreigner settling into a new kingdom. Yet he plainly contributed to the problem, repeatedly acting on his adage that 'money is like muck, not good unless it be spread'. A diplomat observed that 'he takes so much pleasure in giving', and since 'it rarely happens that he does not readily grant whatever is asked', James 'has seriously reduced the royal income'.[5] Frustrated, the king left financial matters to his ministers.

As the fiscal crisis worsened, James's new subjects came to appreciate the more unsettling aspects of his personality. His taste for alcohol became obvious. After a dinner party in 1606, he was grateful that Parliament had not passed a statute against drunkenness because 'otherwise the Justices of the Peace had had much work ado'. His public events were even more disordered. One reportedly was nothing but 'wild riot, excess and devastation of time and temperance'. A ceremony, featuring three ladies performing as Faith, Hope and Charity, abruptly ended when Hope and Faith 'were both sick and spewing'. By that point, James was unable to stand up. He also recoiled from greeting his subjects, a task that Elizabeth had performed admirably, and when he had to touch those afflicted with the 'king's evil' (scrofula), he was visibly uncomfortable.[6]

There was something else that upset him. James was Henry VII's descendant and Elizabeth's heir. But every time he opened his mouth, he also broadcast the fact that he was a foreigner. Consequently, anti-Scottish sentiment flourished during his English reign, something that he could do little to stop. When beset by people, alternately gawking and whispering about 'Jockies' and the 'Scottish elf', his reaction was predictable.[7]

He arrived in Westminster in late April 1603, and three months later the Venetian envoy reported that James 'is lost in bliss', for he 'seems to have almost forgotten that he is a King except in his kingly pursuit of stags'. Peripatetically he wandered from one hunting park to another before returning to three favourites: Royston, Newmarket and Theobalds. With him came a large pack of dogs, a few Scottish attendants and even fewer English ones, who collectively formed what James facetiously termed 'our corporation . . . of fools, horses and dogs'.[8]

The privileged courtiers with daily, intimate access to the king were his Gentlemen of the Bedchamber, and at first they were exclusively old Scottish friends, clearly designed to insulate James from his English attendants. Prominent English aristocrats pressed to join this elite group, but James rejected them all. When he finally relented in 1607 and named an Englishman to this sensitive post, James's logic was obvious to those who knew him. Aside from his handsome appearance, Philip Herbert had only one distinction – a deep knowledge of dogs* and horses.[9]

---

* Herbert was so widely associated with hunting dogs that, in 1649, when he was returned as the County Knight for Berkshire, royalists facetiously lauded this celebrated dog fancier as the logical man to represent 'Bark-shire'.

Safe within this emotional cocoon, James devoted himself to hunting. Once he could not rest before telling a friend that he had just killed 'six hares, a pair of fowls, and a heron'. This passion explains his strange vow to the Earl of Salisbury; when they next met, James promised he would 'halloo to you as freely as to the deepest-mouth hound in all the kennel'.[10]

His enthusiasm for the sport was not widely appreciated. Late in 1603, an anonymous libel charged that he thought he 'had come to the throne for nothing else than to go a-hunting'. In 1604, critics attached a message to James's favourite dog urging him to attend to business, and the Archbishop of York echoed this sentiment. Defiant, James insisted that his health depended on hunting, and, besides, he spent less time hunting than other kings spent 'going to their whores'. It soon became clear that he 'desire[d] to enjoy the chase in the company of very few and with a most private freedom'. Queen Anne rarely joined him.[11]

James was not indolent in the countryside. Couriers kept him connected to Whitehall, and since secretaries, invariably in attendance, often complained about their long hours, James plainly kept them busy. In 1604, he produced *A Counterblast to Tobacco*, condemning it as 'a custom loathsome to the eye, hateful to the Nose, harmful to the brain, dangerous to the Lungs, and in the black stinking fume thereof, nearest resembling the horrible Stygian smoke of the pit that is bottomless'. He also found time for his abiding fascination with witches, though he was becoming more sceptical. In 1605, he persuaded Anne Gunter to confess to having made fraudulent accusations, thus sparing several people from imminent execution.[12] But aside from such diversions, his time was increasingly devoted to weightier issues – Parliament, finances and religion.

His dealings with Parliament were rocky. In addition to being a foreigner in a robustly xenophobic age, James was further hobbled because the same word described two different political institutions, and while the Scottish Parliament was relatively biddable, its English counterpart was not. The power of the Westminster assembly always varied with the monarch's financial need, and as Elizabeth's wars drained the Exchequer, Parliament's authority had increased. It rose higher still as James ran up additional debts. Furthermore, while the political theories he outlined in *The True Law of Free Monarchies* made sense in Scotland, given his struggles with the Kirk, the same notions were unsettling in England. Thus, James's long, learned orations in a distinctive Scots accent generally only succeeded in irritating the Parliament-men, who thought he was disparaging English traditions.

Consider his experience in 1604. When he blocked the return of an outlaw as an MP, a logical action to James's mind, he ended up having to concede that the Commons alone could judge contested elections. He could only watch with mounting frustration as the Lower House refused to pass a new subsidy or, more importantly for him, to act on his proposal to unify the two realms. He won few friends there when he told the Parliament-men: 'I am not of such a stock as to praise fools.'[13] Notwithstanding the Commons' indifference, he tried to make the union a fait accompli by encouraging his Scottish courtiers to take English wives, by adopting the Union Flag and by insisting that he be addressed as the 'King of Great Britain'.

James's fundamental policy was one he had employed in Scotland. His judges should 'use justice upon the obstinate', show 'grace to the penitent, and enlarge them that seem to be a little schooled by the rod of affliction'.[14] The Catholics, however, sorely tested him. Late in her reign, Elizabeth had waged a brutal campaign against Catholics, six of whom had been eviscerated in 1602 and one in February 1603. Since some regarded James's mother as a holy martyr, Catholic expectations rose on his accession, and initially he was more accommodating – until several plots forced him to reconsider.

In July 1603, James learned of two loosely linked plots. The Main Plot, which would have placed his cousin Lady Arabella Stuart on the throne, involved several Catholics as well as Lord Cobham and Sir Walter Raleigh, and the conspirators in the Bye Plot, a Scottish-style royal kidnapping, were almost exclusively Catholic. Shortly afterwards, two Catholics were drawn and quartered in 1604 and two more in 1605. James also banished all Catholic clerics on pain of death.

After his experience with the Kirk, James warmly embraced the Church of England and its learned, deferential clergy. For years in Scotland, James 'had prayed on his knees before every Sermon that he might hear nothing from the Preacher which might grieve him'.[15] In contrast he rarely heard anything even mildly distressing from an English minister. For him, the English Church occupied the *via media*, a moderate position somewhere between Calvinist

Geneva and Catholic Rome that might lead to a general Christian reconciliation. As he constantly reiterated, James thought he faced two equally dangerous foes – Catholics and Puritans, the English version of his old *bêtes noires*, the radical Presbyterians. In response, he instinctively sought to co-opt as many people he could while isolating, and neutralizing, the radicals. Early in 1604, he got his first opportunity to do so.

In response to the Millenary Petition calling for the further reformation of the Church, James summoned leading clerics to the Hampton Court Conference. He was sympathetic to godly ministers who wanted to improve preaching, and in response to valid complaints about flawed English translations of the Bible, he ordered a new, authoritative one. Yet although the petition carefully avoided attacking bishops, James quickly perceived a replay of his earlier disputes with radical Calvinists, and he announced that Scottish Presbyterianism and monarchy went together like God and the devil because 'then Jack, and Tom, and Will, and Dick shall meet and censure me and my Council'. During the discussion, he repeated his aphorism – no bishop, no king. Consequently, Archbishop Bancroft began a campaign to encourage more effective preaching and to force all clerics to subscribe to the Church's basic principles, ultimately depriving eighty nonconformists of their appointments.[16]

These new policies did nothing to soften Catholic opinion. While sceptics then and now might well wonder about the validity of the Main and Bye Plots, there was no doubting the plot that followed these in 1605. This one involved placing the nine-year-old Princess Elizabeth on the throne after a massive explosion vaporized King James, most Protestant aristocrats and hundreds of Parliament-men inside the Palace of Westminster. Only at the last moment, thanks in part to James's thorough investigation, was the Gunpowder Plot detected. Some of the king's Scottish servants first interviewed Guy Fawkes, who allegedly announced that he intended 'to blow you Scotch beggars back to your native mountains'.[17]

Horrified by the idea that he, like his father, might die in an explosion, James responded energetically to the Gunpowder Plot. The executioner duly carved up about twenty Catholics, some for involvement in the plot and others for failing to take the new Oath of Allegiance that James required in the wake of the conspiracy. The plot even persuaded the tight-fisted Parliament-men to approve a new subsidy bill, which brought some £400,000 to the Exchequer. Yet the plot did not initiate an anti-Catholic pogrom. James carefully distinguished the plotters from most Catholics, who, he told Parliament, 'may yet remain good and faithful subjects'.[18] The English Catholics soon learned that James's anger quickly passed, and he did not strictly enforce the penal laws. Yet the plot, which exposed the lax security around the king, could not persuade James, even briefly, to suspend hunting. His fate, he explained, was in God's hands.

After these crises, James reluctantly came to realize that his new realm was much more than a holiday park full of prosperous subjects, fat deer and baubles like the Mirror of Great Britain. He now had to focus on some truly vexatious issues.

4
Parliament Robes

In 1610, a painter captured James in his red velvet Parliament robes and his elegant shoes with rosettes, standing on a Persian carpet with the great 'George' of the Order of the Garter around his neck and jewels in his hat. (See picture 4.) He looks every inch the powerful ruler, and that was exactly the image he needed to convey since he had just summoned the Parliament-men to pass a bold new financial arrangement to stabilize his regime.

* * *

'In this disease I am the patient,' James told his councillors in 1607, 'and ye have promised to be the physicians and to use the best cure upon me.' Cleverly he reappointed most of Elizabeth's ministers, and for the state's institutional memory he could turn to Lord Chancellor Ellesmere and Lord Treasurer Dorset, but, above all, he relied on the Earl of Salisbury, first as Secretary of State and then as treasurer. Ever fond of nicknames, he dubbed the diminutive Salisbury 'my beagle'. Given James's fascination with dogs, it almost verged on praise, and it certainly was better than Elizabeth's name for him – 'my pigmy'.[1]

After the 1604 Hampton Court Conference, James

spent much of his time on religious matters, and here he needed little help. Decades of listening to Scottish ministers had left him with a sincere appreciation of a good sermon. At least twice a week he heard sermons, which he enjoyed analysing. He pored over the published versions, and he delighted in theology disputations. Consequently, as Scottish ministers could have told their English counterparts, James was perfectly capable of interrupting an erring preacher.

The English bishops became James's friends, and he knew them well enough to attach fond labels to many of them. He dubbed Bishop Andrewes of Winchester 'a voice from heaven' and quipped that Bishop King of London was 'the king of preachers'. At mealtimes he discussed theology with them, the more recondite the better, and sometimes, when troubled by his conscience, he summoned them to comfort him at night. When appointing new bishops, he had a simple policy: he advanced preachers he liked. His care extended to those asked to preach at Paul's Cross in the City of London, the most prominent media outlet of the day. He invited the lecturers to discuss their thoughts for the sermon in advance so that he could, as he quipped, tune the pulpits. The task of licensing books he left to the Bishop of London's chaplains, but he regularly monitored the latest works.[2] In short, he took the title of Defender of the Faith seriously.

Admittedly, critics remained. Catholic clerics were still executed in his reign, but the number steadily declined. Likewise the penal laws against Catholics became more of a mere nuisance as James soon backed their lax enforcement – provided each recusant made a financial composition. In 1610 James announced that if Catholics 'be good and quiet Subjects, I hate not their persons'.[3] At the same time, James had no tolerance of separatists who refused to conform to his Church, most of whom (including the future Pilgrim Fathers) went into exile. Yet he only acted in the face of repeated obstinacy. For example, he personally tried to persuade Bartholomew Legate of the error of his heterodox ways, and he only abandoned the effort after Legate admitted that he had not prayed in seven years. James contemptuously dismissed him, 'away, base fellow', and left him to be burned as a heretic.[4]

His personal involvement in ecclesiastical matters soon led to his most daring action. Observers came to expect a steady stream of books and clerics flowing out to James's hunting lodges. But something unusual was plainly going on when James had Cardinal Bellarmine's works read aloud at his meals – all four volumes of them. He was aware that many English Catholics had displayed their loyalty to Elizabeth, and after the various Catholics plots of 1603–5, he saw his new Oath of Allegiance, which explicitly denied the pope's power to depose him, as a way of winnowing loyal Catholics from the more obstinate ones, led by Jesuits. While some Catholics did take the oath, many others followed papal decrees and refused to comply. James therefore decided to attack the papacy itself and its leading controversialist, Cardinal Bellarmine.

Early in 1608, printers struggled to meet James's mammoth order for his latest work, which appeared in multiple Latin and French editions as *Triplici Nodo, Triplex Cuneus* and in English ones as *An Apology for the Oath of Allegiance*. Before a continental audience, James displayed his learning. Casually citing the Bible and the Church Fathers, he rebuked Bellarmine, and by extension the pope, for failing to notice James's repeated favours to his Catholic population. Only repeated plots had compelled him to make a distinction between those 'who although they were otherwise Popishly affected, yet retained in their hearts the print of their natural duty to their Sovereign' and those who were carried away 'with the like fanatical zeal' of the 'Powder-Traitors'.[5]

His book caused a furore. Along with Bishops Barlow and Andrewes, William Barclay, a Scottish lawyer, and John Donne, the English poet, rushed to second James, while a host of Catholic authors attacked him. As Bishop Montague noted: 'there is scarce a People, Language or Nation in Christendom, out of which his Majesty hath not received some answer or other; either by way of refuting, or at least by railing.'[6] Unfortunately for the king, Bellarmine's response highlighted an embarrassing fact: in 1599 James had written a flattering letter to Pope Clement. This in turn prompted the king to convict Lord Balmerino, his secretary, for producing this letter allegedly without James's knowledge, and it led him to issue another tract, his 1609 *Premonition to All Most Mighty Monarchs*, warning of the dangers of the pope's deposing power.

Although battered by this controversy, James could not have been happier. After years of obscurity, he had finally thrust himself into the centre of the continental Republic of Letters. To celebrate his second theological work, he went hunting with his son, Prince Henry. But they galloped so hard that their horses dropped dead from exhaustion, and they had to spend the night in a farmer's cottage, as the courtiers panicked over their disappearance.

More good news came in 1611 when the learned team of biblical scholars completed their new translation and wrote a dedication praising their patron. King James's faith, they maintained, was as apparent 'in the furtherest parts of Christendom by writing in defence of the Truth' as it was at home, and his support of the new translation 'hath so bound and firmly knit the hearts of all your Majesty's loyal and religious people unto you that your very name is precious among them . . . and they bless you in their hearts'. Indeed it seemed obvious that James 'may be the wonder of the world in this latter age'.[7]

While James enjoyed these triumphs, his ministers struggled to contain the ever-widening pool of red ink. They had little success. Parliament was unhelpful because its members adhered to the traditional notion that, in peacetime, the monarch should live on his own resources. Salisbury was able to cut some expenses; in 1611, for example, James only spent £7,442 on jewels, a fifth of what he had spent in 1608. Yet while these budget-cutting exercises certainly helped, the regime's best hope was revenue enhancement.

With peace, the economy had boomed. Early in his reign, the East India Company established a base in Gujarat from which English merchants quickly developed a lucrative commerce not only with the Mughal emperor, but also with the Shah of Persia and the Sultan of Bantam. James also renewed the charters of both the Levant Company and the Spanish Company, whose trade flourished. Furthermore, English colonists landed in Virginia in 1607 and in Bermuda in 1609, and after foundering for several years, the planters soon found a lucrative product, ironically a plant James loathed – tobacco. In Scotland, James had had repeated trouble with the Gaelic-speaking, largely Catholic inhabitants of the Hebrides, and in his frustration he had tried to establish Scottish Protestant colonies there. These proved unsuccessful, but James was able to implement the same policy after the Irish Catholic earls fled Ulster in 1607. He subsequently initiated large-scale Anglo-Scottish Protestant settlements there. Finally, at the end of his reign, his subjects established the first English colony in the Caribbean on St Kitts.[8]

With this surging expansion in trade, Exchequer officials viewed customs duties as the best way to solvency. Late in Elizabeth's reign, she had increased duties on a few imports, one of which was currants. Since the rate had not increased in years, further increases seemed unobjectionable. But the Levant merchants who imported the currants did object because Parliament had not approved the increase, and one of them, John Bate, caused a riot in 1606 over the higher custom duties. In 1608, after the Court of Exchequer considered Bate's case and ruled in favour of the king, James imposed further increases on other imports, and the crown's financial position, while still precarious, improved somewhat.[9] Nevertheless, by 1610 Salisbury was facing a fiscal crisis.

Although he had cut expenditure and increased revenues, Salisbury could not eliminate the annual deficit, which was running at about £160,000. The best solution, he suggested, was for James to don his robes and ask the Parliament-men for immediate financial assistance. The king was less certain. Indeed, he had come to equate Parliament with an interregnum during which he no longer reigned. Nevertheless he agreed to try, and, in a two-hour address, he duly made the case for money to fund possible military intervention in the developing Jülich–Cleves crisis, which threatened to open a general religious war on the continent. In the process, he could not resist the opportunity to badger the Parliament-men about the need for new game laws. After admitting, 'I know you think that I speak partially in this case like a Hunter', he stressed the need to outlaw 'ungentlemanlike' hunting 'at unseasonable times', when, for example, pheasants and partridges 'are no bigger than Mice'.[10]

After an awkward beginning, Salisbury successfully brokered the Great Contract, in which James would surrender feudal levies such as purveyance and wardship in return for a fixed annual subsidy, which rose from £180,000 to £200,000. Talks stalled, however, after the Commons demanded that impositions, the new customs duties, be added to the contract. Apprehensive of the new demands, James began listening to a Scottish courtier, Sir Robert Carr, more than to Salisbury.

These delicate negotiations foundered on increasingly vocal anti-Scottish sentiment. In December 1610, James heard that an anonymous Parliament-man would soon propose that James should 'send home the Scots if I looked for any supply [parliamentary funding]'. No such petition ever emerged, but the rumour only confirmed the anti-Scots prejudice, which was all too present, if generally muted. Englishmen laughed at poetic libels, one of which recounted how avaricious Scotsmen had stolen everything in London, even the lead off Westminster Hall's roof, while another told how England languished as 'the King he hawks and hunts' and 'the Scotts get all by lying'. And even on the London stage, a character in a play ridiculing colonization of Virginia had said about the Scots: 'we should find ten times more comfort of them there than we do here.' The prospect of these insulting comments being openly voiced in Parliament infuriated James. He made a basic fact clear to Salisbury: 'that nation cannot be hated by any that loves me', and if necessary he vowed to print 'the truth that the English have tasted as much and more of my liberality than the Scots have done'.[11]

His mood was not improved after the Parliament-men presented a list of grievances, which he found insultingly long, and after they seemed to compare him to Jehoram, the idolatrous King of Judah. 'Such bold and villainous speeches,' he sputtered, 'ought ever to be crushed in the cradle.' He began calling the Commons 'the House of Hell', complaining that 'our fame and actions have been daily tossed like tennis balls amongst them' and railing that the Parliament-men 'have perilled and annoyed our health, wounded our reputation, emboldened all ill-natured people, encroached upon many of our privileges, and plagued our purse'. He succinctly expressed his attitude to the institution in one line: 'God send us some better comfort after this misery.'[12]

He knew the magnitude of the decision that faced him. But after the new demands in the Great Contract and after the digs about his fellow countrymen and his alleged tyranny, he felt he had no other option. For the time being, he put away his Parliament robes. Late in 1610, since it was obvious that 'there is no more trust to be laid upon this rotten reed of Egypt', James told Salisbury 'to cast your care upon the next best means how to help my state'.[13] Wearily Salisbury, whose deteriorating health soon led to his death, turned to this mammoth task of finding a non-parliamentary solution. In the meantime, James was talking more and more with Carr.

5
Brocades and Lace

James knew how to display his authority using stock props like state robes, jewelled hats and Garter insignia. Around 1615, a painter depicted the king wearing his Garter collar and another fine hat ornament. But these are almost lost amid his stunning clothing with its intricate brocades and delicate lace. (See picture 5.) Never before had he looked so magnificent, and never again would he exhibit such royal splendour. This portrait, like those of William Larkin from the 1610s, illustrates the period of James's greatest excess, which occurred, ironically, as his ministers sought to fulfil his wish and to find 'the next best means how to help my state'.

*   *   *

James's accession in 1603 had come amid personal trage-dies. His eldest children, Henry, Elizabeth and Charles, had been born in 1594, 1596 and 1600 respectively. But a second daughter, born in 1598, had died fourteen months later. Then, in 1602, his third son died shortly after birth, and in 1603 Anne miscarried. Jubilation over the birth of baby girls in 1605 and 1606 proved short-lived as they too died. James and Anne had never been particularly close, and these devastating losses drove them even further apart. Anne had no other pregnancies, and James developed a new emotional outlet.

In 1604, the Earl of Dunbar persuaded James to appoint Robert Carr to a minor bedchamber post, and in 1607, after Carr was injured in a tilting match, the king nursed him and even taught him Latin. The 'straight-limbed, well-favoured, strong-shouldered and smooth-faced' young man soon became James's latest favourite. While we can only speculate about their sexual relationship, the intensity of James's feelings for Carr was unmistakable. The king, one courtier reported, 'leans on his arm, pinches his cheek, [and] smooths his ruffled garments'. Since James 'doth much covet his presence', a knighthood, lands and money soon came his way.[1]

This much had happened before, but in 1611 James did something unusual. By then, embittered by the persistent anti-Scots sentiment and by Parliament's refusal to agree new financial measures, much less to pass the Act of Union, the king's mood had changed, and, as we have seen, the ruler who had once energetically ruled Scotland became more indifferent to the affairs of state. Instead he took Carr into the full public view, making him Viscount Rochester and then Earl of Somerset, Lord High Treasurer of Scotland and Lord Chamberlain and Lord Privy Seal of England. Courtiers fawned over the new favourite, and Lady Frances Howard married him in 1613. This match connected him with her great-uncle the Earl of Northampton, whom Carr succeeded as the Lord Privy Seal; her cousin the Earl of Nottingham the Lord Admiral; and her father the

Earl of Suffolk the Lord Treasurer. Consequently, Somerset and the Howards dominated the middle period of James's English reign.

The king himself ran true to form. While most courtiers wanted him to stay in the spacious Hampton Court Palace or even the comfortable Theobalds House, James preferred the cramped quarters at Royston and Newmarket. As diplomats came to accept that audiences in Whitehall were infrequent and brief, they dreamed of an invitation to join him in the field; indeed, in anticipation, a Spanish envoy ordered a special hunting outfit. But when the invitation came, the experience often proved alarming because, as one ambassador discovered, 'it is not to be believed the amount of fatigue his Majesty will endure in this exercise'. The envoy had to listen as James 'discoursed at large on the chase' and to watch him slaughter two deer. More unsettling still, James insisted that, before dinner, the ambassador had to kill one himself. The king, one observer noted, was determined on 'spending all the time he can upon hunting and studies'.[2]

From the countryside James monitored the latest publications, ordering diplomats to suppress ones that offended him and to discover those responsible for such items. To assist him with his responses, his stable of advisers ran the gamut from Marco Antonio de Dominis, the renegade Catholic Archbishop of Spalato, to George Eglisham, a Scottish controversialist. Chief among them was Isaac Casaubon, the celebrated French scholar. A German visitor watched as Casaubon interrupted James's meal to deliver a document, which the two men then discussed in French and Latin.[3]

The king continued to write. In 1617, James's two
passions – hunting and recreation – came together when
he discovered that godly magistrates in Lancashire had
unilaterally imposed a rigid form of sabbatarianism. He
therefore issued his *Declaration ... Concerning Lawful
Sports*, which authorized pastimes like dancing and
archery on Sunday and a variety of May games. Much
more effort went into his campaign against Conrad Vorstius, a Dutch theologian whose views James regarded as
heretical. In 1611, after having his works burned and after
pressing the Dutch Estates General to dismiss him from his
academic post, James published a declaration against
Vorstius 'to make known to the world publicly in print,
how much we detest such abominable Heresies'. The king
encouraged others to join the assault, and he expected
envoys to have read the work, which he liked to discuss
with them.[4]

His polemics earned him enemies abroad, and while
some responded with scholarly refutations, others simply
reviled him. *Prurit-anus*, an anonymous 1609 tract, con-
flated James's alleged puritanism with the unfortunate
medical condition of an itchy anus, while the German controversialist Scioppius in the same year probed the same
tender spot with *Collyrium Regium* (*The Royal Supposi-
tory*). But worst still was the scandalous 1615 *Corona
Regia*, which identified his favourites: one was 'no less
beautiful than brave', another 'a young man pleasing in
his loveliness' and a third 'a young man of incomparable
beauty'. The tract apologized for 'prying into secrets'
which James hid from 'the gossip of the people'. But he

could not conceal that he was 'feasting [his] eyes with drunken pleasure at banquets, inciting desire with immodest words, caressing cheeks, stealing a kiss, stoking a flame from smoke, so to speak, and extinguishing it in private'. The king, the tract concluded, was only acting on Christ's admonition 'suffer little children to come unto me', for 'you summon boys – the very fair ones in particular – and appreciate the benefactions and miracles of nature in them'.[5] This tract stung James, and his agents spent years tracking down those involved with this scandalous publication. But such audacious attacks only illustrated his growing prominence.

James also tirelessly advocated peacemaking. At home, when seven reputed witches from Leicestershire were hanged in 1616, James personally intervened, and after interviewing five other condemned women, he freed them and rebuked the judges for their credulity. James also laboured to eliminate duelling, effectively continuing his earlier efforts to end blood feuds in Scotland, and in 1614 the royal printer brought out *His Majesty's Edict and Severe Censure against Private Combats*. Abroad, James encouraged reconciliation among Christians, repeatedly calling for a General Council to resolve their differences. In 1609, he helped nudge Spain and its rebellious Dutch provinces to a truce, and he backed a negotiated settlement of the Jülich–Cleves dispute. Throughout, James reiterated his motto, taken from Matthew 5:9, 'Blessed are the peacemakers', and cited I Kings 4:25: 'And Judah and Israel dwelt safely, every man under his vine and under his fig tree, from Dan even to Beersheba.'[6]

Amid these labours James had not forgotten about Scotland, and in 1616 workmen began repairing Edinburgh Castle and Falkland Palace. A proclamation soon came out, strictly banning the hunting of either birds or deer within eight miles of either royal residence. King James was coming home, and he needed ample game. His fellow countrymen were well represented within James's household and on the English Council. Some in England criticized his insistence on balancing factions, since 'it is most harmful that the king has maintained in England the form of government to which he was accustomed in Scotland'.[7] Yet wiser heads knew that James liked to keep his options open. In addition to seeing old friends and revisiting Stirling Castle, his childhood home, James wanted to lobby the General Assembly to approve the Five Articles, which gave bishops an even larger role within the Kirk. The measure was eventually passed in 1618.[8]

In 1616, his public image shone most brightly in *The Works of the Most High and Mighty Prince, James*, which reprinted his prose tracts. As Bishop Montague explained in the preface, obstinate Catholics 'are not safe from being blasted by the breath of his Majesties Books'. Granted, James's position on the Oath of Allegiance had provoked a furious response: 'Good Lord, what a stir we had . . . what a commotion.' But once Catholics in Venice and France had become aware of the corrupting influence of the pope, even they appreciated that 'God hath in this age stirred up Kings to deliver his People from a spiritual Egypt and Babylon'. After citing the newly translated Bible, James's intervention in Scotland, where he 'restored the Bishops there', and the king's commitment to peace and justice, Montague drew the obvious conclusion: 'God hath given us a Solomon.'[9]

The various aspects of the British Solomon's personality were on display during his 1615 visit to Cambridge University. Since he rode from Newmarket, there were few women in his party other than Somerset's new wife. The Latin disputation held in his honour was worthy of a learned ruler – and a huntsman. It concerned 'whether dogs could make syllogisms'. Embarrassed by the topic, the moderator soon halted the proceedings, but James intervened, telling the moderator either to 'think better of his dogs or not so highly of himself'. Next came a Latin play, full of prostitutes and ribald humour, mocking Scioppius and other Catholic critics, the obstinate inhabitants of 'Magna Puritania' and pretentious common lawyers. James was delighted.[10] He soon came back for an encore performance – but only after killing a deer on the way into town.

Notwithstanding this triumphant visit, success in fiscal matters remained as elusive as ever, and James's financial problems worsened. Some at court favoured a closer alignment with France and another parliamentary session. The Howards, however, questioned the institution's utility and instead favoured implementing new fiscal experiments and establishing closer relations with Spain.

In 1614, James half-heartedly tried Parliament again, confessing at the opening that 'I had no great cause to love parliament and my counsel were against' summoning it and warning that 'if for my relief I be forced to stretch my prerogative the world then will see where the fault had been'. Although he predicted that this would be the Parliament of Love, it quickly became, a member observed, the Parliament of Fear. James was angry that Parliament wanted him to declare 'that all impositions [new increases in customs duties] are unjust without consent of parliament', something James would rather 'die a 100 deaths' than ever do. The tension only increased with complaints that 'we have nothing but ill examples of all riot and dissoluteness' at court and with calls 'to send all strangers [i.e. Scotsmen] home'. He soon dissolved the session.[11]

Aside from this ill-fated meeting, he ruled without Parliament during the 1610s as he explored new revenue schemes with the Howards. He cheerfully sold anything of value. From 1611 he awarded a baronetcy, a hereditary knighthood, to any gentleman able to pay £1,095, a scheme that produced £90,885 in three years. Likewise he took to selling peerages, with an English barony fetching £10,000 and an English earldom £20,000. Bargain hunters could often be tempted by deeply discounted Irish titles. He even released Walter Raleigh from the Tower to find the fabulous mines of El Dorado – provided he did not harm any Spaniards in the process.[12]

More extreme revenue enhancements followed. The Commons had long opposed royal monopolies and impositions, but with Parliament out of the picture, James authorized new patents and increases in the customs rates. Furthermore, desperate for ready cash, James in 1616 accepted £200,000 to retire the entire debt of £618,000 that the Dutch Republic owed England. In the hope of earning a windfall profit, James even implemented

1. In this portrait of James as an eight-year-old, he already displays a precocious interest in hunting, which soon became his passion.

IACOBVS · 6 · D · G · R ·
SCOTORVM
ÆTA · 29 ·
1595 ·

2. The expensive furs and fabrics and, above all, the jewelled hat
project the confident authority of the twenty-nine-year-old King
of Scotland.

3. In John de Critz's painting from 1604, the restrained dress of the new King of England only emphasizes his extravagant hat jewel, the famous 'Mirror of Great Britain'.

4. This anonymous portrait depicts the middle-aged King of England wearing his state clothes and the great 'George' of the Order of the Garter, a resplendent outfit he wore for parliamentary ceremonies.

5. Although the mature king generally favoured sombre clothing, he appears here in truly sumptuous attire, typical of the excesses of his court in the 1610s.

6. In Paul van Somer's 1618 painting, the armour around
the throat and at the feet of Rex Pacificus illustrate the rising
continental tensions.

7. This remarkable, if little known, portrait vividly captures the aged
monarch towards the end of his life.

8. In the central panel of Rubens' ceiling for the Banqueting House, angels escort James into heaven.

Alderman Cockayne's radical scheme to alter the cloth trade by cutting the Dutch out of dyeing and finishing English cloth, the realm's chief export. The experiment proved disastrous, and James eventually reverted to the status quo. Not surprisingly, a contemporary joke held that the fastest way to bankrupt Spain would be for King Philip to appoint James's financial officials. Meanwhile, the debt inexorably rose, reaching nearly £700,000 by 1617.

His crumbling finances enraged James. Since he did not have a head for numbers, he appointed commission after commission to advise him, and he chided them in 1617: 'why are ye councillors, if ye offer no counsel?'[13] Yet nothing improved. James could console himself that the other rulers faced similar problems. In 1607, for example, Philip III of Spain had been forced to declare bankruptcy. Amid these controversial schemes, James focused on his family. But there he only found more grief.

At the end of 1612 James was expansive. His daughter Elizabeth was about to marry the Elector Frederick V of the Palatinate, a leading German Protestant ruler. But just as the bridegroom arrived, James's eldest son, Henry, fell seriously ill. Although father and son had got along well enough, tensions between them had become increasingly evident. Henry thought his father's hunting excessive, while James lamented that his son was no sportsman, and in statecraft Henry favoured France and Parliament, while his father sided with Spain and the Howards. None the less, Henry was his son. Unable to bear the sight of him dying, James left for Theobalds because he found 'the solitude of the country more fitting for grief and tears than the bustle of London and the Court'. For weeks following the death of his eldest son, James muttered: 'Henry is dead, Henry is dead.'[14] His depression in turn triggered a serious bout of nephritis, which forced him to take to his bed.

Ugly rumours circulated that Henry had been poisoned, and to allay these suspicions, royal doctors conducted an autopsy and found nothing unusual. Yet undoubtedly Sir Thomas Overbury, the Earl of Somerset's confidential adviser, had been poisoned. He had mysteriously died late in 1613, but the solid evidence of poisoning only emerged in September 1615. James's response was uncompromising. He reportedly 'fell down on his knees, and prayed God that his curse might fall upon him and his posterity, if he would pardon or spare any person whatsoever that could be found guilty thereof'.[15] The investigation promptly led to some predictably shady characters – and then to the Earl and Countess of Somerset.

The lurid affair exceeded anything on the London stage. Overbury had guided Somerset's career until the two fell out over the favourite's new wife. Because Frances Howard was married to the Earl of Essex when she began her affair with Somerset, she requested a divorce in 1613 on the grounds that witchcraft had made her husband impotent. Contemporaries reacted to the allegation with profound scepticism. Nevertheless, James quietly supported the divorce, which was granted in September 1613. Two months later James presided over, and paid for, their marriage.

The scandalous divorce generated bawdy comments about the countess's virginity. Worse soon followed. Because Overbury had opposed the divorce, she had him poisoned with a mercury enema lest he expose secret details. The countess eventually made a full confession, carefully exculpating her husband. For his part, he loudly maintained his innocence, though his performance in the courtroom was unpersuasive. The court quickly found the couple, and her accomplices, guilty of murder.

This verdict presented James with the most controversial decision of his reign. His relationship with Somerset had already become turbulent as the king was involved with another man. Somerset responded with 'mad fits', alternating 'dogged sullenness' with 'loud speaking', and James criticized him for his 'long creeping back and withdrawing yourself from lying in my chamber, notwithstanding my many hundred times earnest soliciting you to the contrary'. James prided himself on his loyalty, and Somerset was his most 'inwardly trusty friend and servant'. Furthermore, having acted as James's confidential secretary, he knew many state secrets, not the least of which concerned his divorce. Vowing to consider 'first my conscience before God, and next my reputation in the eyes of the whole world', James pressed Somerset to confess 'if there be a spark of grace left in him'.[16] There was not, and Somerset refused to co-operate, although a confession would have made a pardon easier and forestalled a public trial and further revelations.

As James wavered, public expectations ran strongly in favour of execution, especially after one of the countess's accomplices prayed before he was hanged that 'the judges would not make a net to catch the little fishes and let the great ones go'. Meanwhile, the couple's friends argued for mercy, citing her confession and the circumstantial evidence against him. In the end, James could not simply let them be executed. Instead they remained in the Tower. In 1622, James sent them, not to the gallows, but to their rural estate under house arrest, and in 1624 he pardoned them altogether. Above all else he valued loyalty; he had earlier told Salisbury: 'all that know me do know that I never use to change my affections from any man except the cause be printed on his forehead.' Plainly he found Somerset's brow clean enough. Many others thought differently. After his decision, a crowd followed a coach reportedly carrying the couple and their attendants through London, 'railing and reviling . . . putting them all in great fear'.[17]

After this astonishing outcome, many found James's speech in the Star Chamber a few days later positively breathtaking. He asked them to recall 'how impartial I have been in declaring of Law', and he announced that 'if any man moved me to delay Justice, that it was against the Office of a King so to do'.[18] His reasoning in the Overbury case reveals that, for him, affection edged out justice, albeit narrowly.

The rest of the Howards escaped the net that caught the countess, but their influence was dwindling. Northampton died in 1614, and Nottingham was effectively incapacitated by illness. In 1618, fate finally caught up with the countess's father, Lord Treasurer Suffolk. At Audley End, he had erected one of the most lavish 'prodigal' houses of the era. When James visited it in 1614, he reportedly quipped that it was too grand for a king, but might do for a Lord Treasurer. Any humour vanished four years later when it was discovered that Suffolk had financed it, and his lavish lifestyle, by defrauding the Exchequer. James banished him from court and fined him £30,000.

These debacles ruined Somerset and the Howards. It also upset James and besmirched his reputation. About this time, for instance, a manuscript poem deriding his rule employed a striking phrase to describe the state, one that alluded both to the king's loftiest goal and to his alleged sexual proclivities – 'Sodom Britain'.[19] But, isolated in the country, he weathered the shock well enough. After all, he had found another favourite.

6
Gorget and Armour

Paul van Somer's portrait of King James standing next to his crown, sceptre and orb initially seems regal, if a little routine. But then something unusual comes into view. The king has a plate-metal gorget around his neck with the rest of his armour stacked at his feet. (See picture 6.)

The painting reminds the viewer that the man who then described himself as *Rex Pacificus* had earlier led troops against Scottish rebels, and a closer examination of his rhetoric about the blessings of peace reveals an important qualification. In 1604, James assured Parliament that he would not break the peace – 'except I be forced thereunto for the honour of the kingdom or else by necessity'.[1] In 1618, the year Somer painted the picture, continental developments had prompted the king to take the extraordinary step of donning a gorget. The message was clear: James would put on the rest of his armour and go to war if honour and necessity ever required it.

* * *

While his passion for hunting remained, James was plainly ageing, and reports circulated of grooms running on either side of him, holding the reins. Nevertheless, 'nothing is easier than to divert him from doing anything,' the Venetian ambassador noted in 1622, 'than to propose hunting.' James 'has long been accustomed to remain in retirement in remote places of which he is very fond, free and enjoying himself, without pomp or gravity'. The sprawling conflict that would soon engulf James, and the continent, only intensified his devotion to rural sports. In 1620, Roman observers were astonished that James had 'no thought of anything but his hunting', and in 1623, when his councillors urged the king to stay near London, he went to Newmarket and ordered them not to join him there without an invitation. Consequently there was little exaggeration in the 1622 report that 'he goes hunting every day'.[2]

Hunting helped ease the pain of Somerset's fall from grace; so too did George Villiers. In 1614 this younger son of an obscure gentleman only had one shabby suit, but his fortunes dramatically improved after he met King James – predictably enough, in the kennels. This clever, attractive man, and his impudent manner, delighted James. 'If I speak,' he told the king, 'I must be saucy.' He teased James about his 'well shaped legs', and he traded scatological references with the king. The new favourite once wrote that the French had 'shitten mouths', adding 'I pray you, sir, do not kiss that word', and the two amused themselves with a rude abbreviation of countesses – 'cunts'. James promptly became his 'dear dad', and Villiers, again playing to the king's canine enthusiasm, was 'your humble slave and dog'.[3] The king lavished offices, titles and even an aristocratic wife on the young man, who eventually became the Duke of Buckingham.

Publicly, Buckingham was the king's private secretary responsible, James said, for 'keeping my back unbroken with business'. He seemed to be everywhere. After James appointed him Lord Admiral, Buckingham swiftly re-formed the navy, and in 1619 when James published *A Meditation*, comparing Christ's crucifixion to a monarch's labours, he thanked Buckingham in the dedication for his help. Privately he had the king's heart. While we do not know what happened when they were alone, they certainly wrote about nights spent tumbling in bed, and James spoke of his longing to 'see thy white teeth shine upon me', begging his favourite to make 'haste to thy dear dad'. For his part, Buckingham praised James for having shown him 'more affection than between lovers', even than between 'man and wife'.[4] In short order, James's family expanded to include Buckingham and his kin.

This new relationship helped James through several crises, the first of which was Queen Anne's death in 1619. Although they had lived separate lives, James always honoured her, and in a poem he linked her death to the appearance of a comet. 'She is chang'd not dead,' he wrote, for 'no good prince dies / But like the day-star only sets to rise.'[5] Her passing brought on deep depression, just as Prince Henry's death had, and another attack of nephritis. Feverish with loose bowels, at times frothing at the mouth and at others vomiting, James seemed to be dying. Buckingham faithfully nursed him, and the privy councillors gathered to witness his demise, but his condition improved after he passed three stones. To recuperate he went to Theobalds, but he refused to rest until he had inspected the local deer herd.

His grief over Anne paled before the sorrow that his daughter brought him. Shortly after Prince Henry's death, Princess Elizabeth had married the Elector Frederick. She loved her father, lauding him in 1613 as 'the flower of princes, the King of fathers, the best and most gracious father under the sun', and he was delighted as she presented him with grandsons, who ensured the dynasty's future. But in 1619 the cosy intimacy between them ended when Elizabeth and her husband suddenly accepted the Bohemian crown. Although she entreated him 'always to love me', their relationship subsequently became profoundly complicated.[6]

The constitutional situation in Bohemia made James very uneasy. The Estates, which elected their monarch, had first picked the Habsburg archduke Ferdinand in 1617 and then deposed him in 1618, naming Frederick as its next choice. As James explained to Parliament, 'I know not the laws of Bohemia', and even if he did, he detested the idea of crowns being tossed 'like tennis balls'. Equally alarming were the political repercussions. Because Ferdinand soon become the Holy Roman Emperor and his cousin was the King of Spain, Frederick and Elizabeth now faced powerful Habsburg forces in both Bohemia and the Palatinate. Anxiously, Elizabeth begged her father to believe that 'there is only Your Majesty after God from whom we can expect help'.[7]

Although the couple had broad support in England, particularly among the godly, James was extremely wary. He was, if nothing else, a realist, and any interest in military options vanished after a careful report set the price tag for a large British army operating in central Europe at some £800,000 annually, an amount roughly equal to the crown's debt. While Parliament might help, James was leery of re-entering the 'House of Hell'; and to avoid that, he sent token Anglo-Scottish forces to Prague and to Heidelberg, their expenses being defrayed by voluntary contributions at home and by a Danish loan. Elizabeth asked to return to England, a plan that James blocked, fearful of her popularity. Instead, as a sop, he sent her a favourite bed and a monthly pension of £1,000.

Some called for reviving the Elizabethan war against Spain. James, however, knew that the royal navy, his only real asset, could not sail up the Rhine, and because Catholics outnumbered Protestants on the continent, he was fearful of initiating a war of religion. Yet he saw a possible solution. Hitherto plans to marry one of his sons to a Spanish princess had always foundered on religious issues. With the continental crisis James relaunched the idea, offering his sole surviving son, Charles, and this time he was willing to accept an informal religious toleration for the English Catholics, provided the wedding brought Frederick and Elizabeth safely back to the Palatinate.

The veteran Spanish diplomat the Count of Gondomar encouraged James to pursue a negotiated settlement. An easy-going man without the characteristic Spanish gravity, he shared James's fondness for hunting and jokes. Indeed he vied with James 'in putting his hands in the blood of bucks and stags, doing cheerfully everything that his Majesty does'. As James pressed for a Spanish match, he also tried to advertise England's usefulness. He sent a naval squadron to attack the Muslim pirates in Morocco, the common foe of both nations, and sold prized English cannons to Spain, even though they might soon be used against Frederick and Elizabeth.[8]

Although James's response led to mounting criticism at home, he ignored it because he knew that his precarious finances sharply limited any military assistance that he could give to Frederick and Elizabeth. It is hard not to sympathize with him. Just as he had recovered from a serious illness, his daughter and son-in-law had rashly caused this furore, and now he was pressed to take more decisive action, which he believed would be disastrous. In August 1620, he told the Venetian ambassador that 'he did not know what he could do'. He was 'utterly weary' of these vexatious issues, and he hated 'being obliged to spend time over unpleasant matters'. He then exploded: 'I am not God Almighty.' His powerlessness became obvious in November 1620 when Frederick's defeat at the Battle of White Mountain drove him out of Bohemia and threatened to pull James in. Given his well-known devotion to the sport, James's reaction to the news stunned contemporaries; although Newmarket was then full of game, he stopped hunting and forbade anyone else to hunt, muttering that 'he clearly foresaw these disasters'.[9]

Bereft of viable options, he summoned Parliament, and to forestall trouble, he asked the voters to shun 'discontented Persons that cannot fish but in troubled waters'. In his opening address James revealed his bruised feelings, complaining that his previous speeches had turned 'like spittle against the wind upon mine own face'. Yet he need not have worried. After warning against discussing the Spanish match, he told Parliament that if he could not peacefully restore the Palatinate, 'my crown and my blood and the blood of my son shall not be spared for it'. The Commons immediately voted him £160,000. Then, in June, as they adjourned, the members unanimously pledged their 'lives and estates . . . for the maintenance of the cause of God and his Majesty's issue'.[10]

Although the Commons subsequently attacked corruption, impeached Lord Chancellor Bacon and closed down several monopolies, James was delighted, proclaiming: 'never a Lower House showed more respect unto their king than the Common House this Parliament have done unto me.'[11] Unfortunately, he was soon forced to revise his opinion.

In mid 1621, James's chief diplomat came to realize that while the Spanish Habsburgs supported James's negotiations, the Austrian Habsburgs were overrunning the Palatinate. The news led James to request emergency funding to defend Heidelberg. But after the Parliament-men interpreted a motion from one of Buckingham's clients to mean that all restrictions on free debate had been lifted, they denounced a Spanish match and called for a general war against the Habsburgs. Prince Charles sputtered, Gondomar protested and James thundered.

In the first session of Parliament that year, the king had vowed not 'to weary myself or you with such tedious discourses as I have done heretofore'. But he returned to type when, to James's horror, 'some fiery and popular spirits' in the Commons began to morph into his bogeymen.

Anxious to 'usurp upon Our Prerogative Royal', the 'Tribunitial Orators' of the Lower House came to resemble, in his view, both 'the Puritan Ministers in Scotland', who sought to 'bring all kind of causes within the compass of their jurisdiction', and the Jesuits, who used 'Bellarmine's distinction of the Pope's power over all Kings' to claim 'all temporal jurisdiction'. Because the members recommended 'a public war of Religion through all the world' without considering 'how hard and dangerous a task it would prove', he dissolved the session.[12]

The dissolution sharply reduced his options. Without a new subsidy bill, he could not pay the few troops he had in the Palatinate, much less reinforce them. He could only play for time and hope a Spanish match eventually restored Frederick and Elizabeth. To hasten the marriage, he suspended the penal laws against English Catholics in 1622.

While Catholics rejoiced, Protestants fumed. Bold ministers attacked his policy, and an anonymous tract acknowledged that James was the Defender of the Faith and then rudely asked which faith he was defending. Undeterred, James responded vigorously just as he had with radicals in the Kirk. He had supported Lancelot Andrewes and Richard Neile, bishops who opposed the prevailing moderate Calvinism within the Church, and to counteract godly militants, James had begun favouring protégés of Andrewes and Neile, such as William Laud, the new Bishop of St David's. In addition, James issued his *Directions Concerning Preaching*, which put an end to afternoon sermons altogether and banned the morning ones from commenting upon affairs of state. For good measure, he ordered the gentry, many of whom were then enjoying the pleasures of metropolitan life, to return to the countryside, and to ease the pain he wrote a poem assuring upset ladies that 'your husbands will as kindly you embrace / without your jewels or your painted face'.[13]

By the end of 1622, James had tightened his grip on the country – until foreign developments again swept him off balance. His troops flying the English flag still garrisoned three cities in the Palatinate, but in September imperial soldiers stormed Heidelberg and killed the English commander. Enraged, the Privy Council demanded that the Spaniards withdraw or face war. James agreed, but, along with the ultimatum, he sent a more accommodating private message. The Spaniards embraced it, vowing to accelerate the marriage of Prince Charles and the infanta. A family crisis, however, then erupted.

Unlike his relationship with Prince Henry, James had got on well with his younger son, Charles. But late in 1622 the prince announced his plan to go to Madrid, just as James had gone to Copenhagen, vowing to return either with his new Spanish bride or with definite proof of Spanish duplicity. After Buckingham sided with Charles, James did 'nothing but weep and mourn'. He went alone to where he had always found peace – a hunting park – with 'the tears trickling down my cheeks'. Reluctantly he agreed, pledging that 'if my baby's credit in Spain mend not these things [regarding the Palatinate], I will bid farewell to peace in Christendom during our times'.[14]

Charles and Buckingham left early in 1623, disguised en route as Jack and Tom Smith, and the trip, which James termed 'a new romance', initially went well. To impress the Spaniards with the dynasty's grandeur, the king sent Charles and the duke several of his favourite jewels – the 'Three Brethren' and the 'Mirror of France' – and their Garter robes, for on St George's Day it would 'be a goodly sight for the Spaniards to see my boys dine in them'. He was delighted when the Spaniards responded by sending him an elephant for his menagerie. Writing to his son, James explained that he had little fear for Charles's personal safety because the Spaniards could only 'wish you and yours rather to succeed unto me' instead of Elizabeth. Fretting over the hot weather, James warned Charles and Buckingham to 'put not yourselves in hazard by any violent exercise'. Throughout their journey, he wore Buckingham's miniature portrait next to his heart.[15]

The expedition terrified the godly, who feared Charles's conversion, and, in response, James wrote two poems. One lightheartedly urged his anxious subjects to 'Remit the Care, to Royal Pan / of Jack his son, and Tom his man'. The second warned them to 'hold your prattling, spare your pen' because 'If proclamations will not serve / I must do more . . . to keep all in obedience'.[16] Yet this bluff confidence could not mask his growing alarm.

The trip's expense brought the king close to bankruptcy, and, in April, Buckingham annoyed him by refusing to come back as he ordered. Yet the real stumbling block was the English Catholics; James offered a de facto toleration, but the Spanish insisted on a formal one. In March, when the papal nuncio played what James called 'a cooling card', he quoted 'a passage in my book against Bellarmine'. In

May, he reluctantly gave Charles full powers to negotiate, reminding him 'never [to] promise in my name but what may stand with my conscience, honour and safety'. As the Spanish demands escalated, James told his son and favourite that the negotiations 'shall very much shorten my days' – he predicted he would be dead in a few months – for 'I am the more perplexed that I know not how to satisfy the people's expectations here, neither know I what to say to our Council'. Indeed, he regretted the entire trip: 'I now repent me sore that ever I suffered you to go away.'[17] Yet James would agree to anything, provided his boys came home either with or without the infanta.

In early October, they finally returned – alone. The country erupted in widespread celebration, and James rejoiced at their safe arrival. Yet what would he do about the Palatinate?

7
An Old Man and a New Marriage

About the time of Charles and Buckingham's return, James sat for another portrait, wearing a favoured stock item – the lesser 'George' of the Order of the Garter. The truly striking aspect of the painting, however, is James himself. He looks greyer, thicker and puffier. (See picture 7.)

Signs of the king's ageing were everywhere at this point. He had to use a stamp to sign documents; he rested in specially constructed folding furniture while out hunting; and he ordered doorways widened so he could be carried through. Meanwhile, he was increasingly more likely to nap, to play cards or to watch his falcons hunt than to chase deer. Yet he remained alert, and in his final weeks as crises piled one atop the other and the doctors gathered around him, he gave a master class in kingcraft. Indeed, even in his declining state, he was keen to discuss remarriage.

* * *

The reunion of James, Charles and Buckingham was heartfelt. They were devoted to one another and to an idyllic rural life. Unfortunately, they soon fell out. Charles returned formally betrothed to the infanta, whom he now refused to marry, and the emperor had by then overrun the entire Palatinate and transferred Frederick's authority as an imperial elector to the Duke of Bavaria.

In response James wanted to renegotiate, linking the marriage treaty directly to the Palatinate. Charles and Buckingham rejected the idea, arguing that the Spaniards would never restore Frederick and Elizabeth, and when James stressed his poverty, the royal debt having risen to nearly a million pounds, they urged him to summon Parliament. He stressed the insanity of attacking Spain without powerful allies, and they retorted that Louis XIII had an unmarried sister and a large underemployed army. Their loud discussions were themselves novel. Generally James would not brook dissent. But with such limited policy options, he found it difficult to shout down two men he loved.

The Earl of Kellie, who had grown up with the king at Stirling Castle, then presided over the bedchamber, and his letters to his cousin the Earl of Mar reveal the turmoil. Ten days after Charles and Buckingham had returned, Kellie warned that Mar might soon have to choose between the father and the son. In late October, he reported that James was 'much distempered'; on 4 November, 'you cannot imagine . . . the vexation his Majesty has in his mind'; and on 11 November, the king 'is in much trouble in his mind'.[1]

Their debate soon spilled into the Privy Council and eventually into Parliament. There James at times seemed shaken – and with good reason. All of his skill at wriggling out of crises with clever compromises and adroit policy recalculations had plainly failed to resolve the plight of his daughter and son-in-law. Consequently his opening address was uncharacteristically terse, and he likened himself alternately to a traveller just emerging from a heavy mist and to a man waking out of a dream. His statements ranged from pathetic – 'I pray you judge Me charitably' – to delusional: 'you know in your Consciences, that, of all the Kings that ever were, I dare say, never king was better beloved.'[2] By then, it was abundantly obvious that the peaceful solution that James had so doggedly pursued had eluded him. In 1621, he had dissolved Parliament rather than permit a discussion of the Spanish match. Now he formally asked for advice about it, and when Parliament urged him to end the Anglo-Spanish negotiations, he did so.

Flashes of the older, more combative James sometimes reappeared, but his performance in the 1624 Parliament was so different that many contemporaries, and some scholars, have assumed that he had ceded power to Charles and Buckingham. The notion would have elicited bitter laughter from the prince and the duke. Admittedly, for the last eighteen months of his life James was not much in evidence at court. But he never had been, preferring a rural life. Charles and the duke indeed began to conduct parliamentary and diplomatic business – but only within James's strict guidelines.

In Parliament, Charles and Buckingham steered discussion away from a Spanish war, which would have led the Commons over James's tripwire, triggering another dissolution. The duke begged James to relent: 'for so long as you waver between the Spaniards and your subjects to make advantage of both, you are sure to do it with neither.'[3] James ignored him. Consequently, at Charles's insistence the House approved subsidies, not for a war, but for preliminary measures, such as repairing the fleet and coastal fortifications and assisting the Dutch.

James's differences with Charles and Buckingham became increasingly open. While they sided with the godly, he patronized their opponents, including Richard Montague, an Arminian controversialist. Furthermore, although James ended the Spanish negotiations, he welcomed new ones, much to Charles and Buckingham's horror. More importantly, while he would happily ally with Venice, Savoy and the Dutch Republic, he would only go to war if, and only if, Louis XIII joined him, because only the Bourbon military could really match that of the Habsburgs. The French in turn would happily discuss an Anglo-French military league, but only after Charles had married Louis's sister, and these marriage talks then quickly became entangled with the vexed question of Catholic toleration. Deeply frustrated, Charles and Buckingham found James's restrictions as intractable as the immutable laws of the Medes and Persians.

Geopolitics became intensely personal in April 1624 when Spanish agents secretly informed James of a conspiracy that was both plausible and appalling. His favourite's alliance with his son irritated James, who grumbled that, since their return, Buckingham 'had (he knew not how many) Devils within him'. The Spanish allegation played on his anxiety by reporting that Charles and Buckingham were planning a coup d'état that would have James 'confined to his Country House and Pastimes'.[4]

The accusation triggered a family meltdown. James would not let the duke in his carriage, and the prince closeted himself in his room. Buckingham then collapsed, his skin jaundiced and covered with pustules. Medical reports that he was gravely ill abruptly changed the situation. James set guards to see that the duke was undisturbed, and he visited him, sending doctors, medicines and delicacies. Meanwhile, his favourite grovelled. To soothe James's anger, he even redefined popularity: 'were not only all your people, but all the world besides, set together on one side, and you alone on the other, I should, to obey and please you, nay despise all them, and this shall be ever my popularity.' Their reconciliation took place in June, when Buckingham fell to his knees before James with 'his hat off and his hands up'. With tears running down his cheeks, the king said: 'Steenie, I pray God either to recover thee of this sickness or else to transfer the same upon me, as one that would stand in the gap for thee.' His actions were even more eloquent: he hung on Buckingham's neck and covered him 'with one hundred kisses'.[5]

The relationship of the three men quickly returned to normal. James withdrew to the country, where he characteristically reported finding 'a great store of game' and 'the finest company of young hounds that ever was seen'.[6] He left Charles and the duke to handle business and to abide by his restrictions, and after the Spanish allegation they were unlikely to violate them. The negotiations for a French bride quickly advanced, and in late 1624 Louis and

James agreed to an Anglo-French expedition of 15,000 men, whom Count Mansfeld, a German military commander formerly in Frederick's service, would march across northern France and into the Palatinate. After this joint effort and Charles's marriage to Henrietta Maria, a formal military league seemed imminent.

In these talks, Charles and Buckingham were highly visible, but James remained in control – as the French discovered when it came time to sign the marriage treaty in December 1624. James was then in Newmarket, and rather than riding down the sloppy roads to Westminster, he made the French delegation meet him in Cambridge.

As this turbulent year came to an end, James wrote a short letter to Buckingham that allows us to peer into his emotional life. The king made a striking proposal, praying to God that 'we may make at this Christmas a new marriage ever to be kept hereafter'. Towards that end, James confessed: 'I desire only to live in this world for your sake.' Indeed, 'I had rather live banished to any part of the earth with you than live a sorrowful widow's life without you.' He first signed it 'your dad and master', but then struck through the last word and added 'husband'.[7] Granted the term 'widow' had yet to acquire an exclusively female connotation, and 'husband' could refer to the head of a household. Nevertheless this emotional letter testified to the king's eagerness to re-establish close bonds with – even to marry – his favourite.

With couriers almost daily reporting on the French marriage and Mansfeld's progress, Charles and Buckingham begged James to move closer to London. He did so very slowly, arriving on 1 March 1625 at Theobalds, a dozen miles from Whitehall. There he found his son and his favourite fretting over his restrictions.

The Mansfeld project had gone off the rails. In December, as the English troops boarded their transports, the French unilaterally shifted the rendezvous from Calais to Zeeland from where, they hoped, the men would relieve Breda, the vital Dutch border fortress the Spanish were besieging. Grudgingly, Charles and Buckingham agreed. James, however, did not. Because the French cavalry would not arrive in the Netherlands for months, the king feared a French plan to manoeuvre him into a Spanish war while they remained at peace. Consequently he expressly commanded his men to proceed to Heidelberg.

His decision ignored some nasty realities. Without a cavalry escort, the English infantry would be slaughtered, and without funds – the Exchequer was then empty – the troops would starve, since the Dutch understandably saw no need to feed soldiers who would not help them. Greatly agitated, Charles and Buckingham pleaded with James to change his mind, lest this project squander nearly £200,000 and 12,000 Englishmen, as well as ruining Buckingham's relations with the Commons. Nevertheless James refused to relent, and Mansfeld's English force rapidly dissipated.

Meanwhile Gondomar, who had left London in 1622, was making his way back from Spain to London, where James planned to greet him warmly because the count had promised to bring a resolution to the Palatinate question. Buckingham was horrified. Having publicly denounced Philip IV and his ministers in Parliament, he was unlikely to survive an Anglo-Spanish rapprochement. Luckily for the duke, Gondomar was by then very ill and moving slowly. Yet nothing Buckingham could say or do could persuade James to withdraw his invitation.[8]

At the height of these crises, James himself fell ill in early March. He had what contemporaries called a tertian ague, most likely a form of malaria, then common in marshy East Anglia. While not normally fatal, the ague might bring on unpredictable complications, given the king's existing ailments, and James was depressed after fever had recently claimed the life of his relative the Marquis of Hamilton. His doctors tried to keep him comfortable as he alternately shivered and sweated. To pass the time, he played cards with Buckingham, and to raise his spirits, his attendants brought in a litter of terrier puppies who delighted James by leaping on his bed.

A mundane episode of royal illness suddenly became alarming in mid March when the king's doctors returned from dinner to find that, without their knowledge, Buckingham and his mother had applied plasters to James's chest and wrists. In the spring, when Buckingham had contracted the same ailment, he had made a good recovery after the application of plasters by a local doctor; hence he tried the same treatment on James. The king's doctors removed the plasters, however, and reiterated that they alone should treat James. Because the treatment had no ill effect on the king, the incident would have been forgotten if Buckingham had not intervened again.

By the night of 20/21 March, James had improved so much that his staff talked about moving him to Hampton Court. But then Buckingham and his mother reapplied plasters, and they also mixed a white powder into a glass of wine, which James drank. This time the king immediately complained about the treatment, and a few attendants began muttering darkly about poison, which prompted the duke to explode. Meanwhile James swiftly declined. Yet even in his final hours, after a stroke left him speechless, he still ran to true to form: he signalled for a book to read. He died shortly afterwards on 27 March 1625.

Immediately after his death, Charles lifted the restriction on Mansfeld's movement and disinvited Gondomar. In addition, Buckingham gave the doctors a list of the ingredients in the plasters and potion and asked them to sign a statement that he had given James nothing harmful. They declined; they did not know what had actually been in the remedies.

The extraordinary circumstances of James's death generated three different narratives. The traditional 'good death' account emphasized his piety. After asking forgiveness of those he had offended and freely forgiving all others, he received communion as Charles and Buckingham wept. His final hours were spent in prayer, and even after his stroke he signalled his assent to questions by blinking his eyes.

Much more dramatic was an account published in 1626. In it, George Eglisham, a royal doctor who had not been present at Theobalds, alleged that Buckingham had poisoned the king to forestall Gondomar's arrival. Its emotional highpoint came with James's exclamation: 'Oh this white powder! would to God I had not taken it, it will cost my life.' Prompted by Eglisham's pamphlet, the 1626 Parliament investigated James's death, and in defending his action, Buckingham offered another poignant detail. Overhearing talk of poisoning, James reportedly said: 'they are worse than devils that say it.'[9]

Although Charles himself never responded to Eglisham, his supporters did after Parliament suggested in 1648 that Charles had been involved in his father's murder. They offered the third narrative of James's last days. After communion, James said to his favourite: 'Steny, I am willing to die but am sorry I must leave the World before I have done for thee [what] my love intended.'[10] The king then died in Buckingham's arms. The duke was weeping so much that he could not see to close James's eyes. The servant, who helped him do so, was still alive in 1648, offering to answer questions about the scene at Theobalds.

We will never know the precise details of James's death. He may have been poisoned, but for many reasons this seems unlikely. Buckingham's second medical intervention, however, may well have inadvertently compromised his health.

However the old king died, his son unquestionably gave him the largest funeral the country had ever seen, and he walked beside his coffin from Somerset House to Westminster Abbey. The mourning for King James, it must be conceded, was generally more perfunctory than heartfelt. At the time, Charles and even Buckingham were more popular than the querulous old king. Yet while most received the news of his death with dry eyes, a few were sobbing. Predictably they were James's huntsmen.

Conclusion
The Phoenix King

Those seeking the grand tomb of the first Stuart monarch will be disappointed. James I's body is where his son left it – sharing a crypt with Henry VII in the Lady Chapel of Westminster Abbey. But Charles had not forgotten his father. Although less eloquent, Charles had a better visual sense than his father, and because he commissioned Rubens to paint the ceiling of the Banqueting House, James VI and I can still be seen in the central panel, ascending to heaven. (See picture 8.) The old king seems a little surprised. But on reflection, he certainly merits more acclaim than he has received.

* * *

James's failures have dominated assessments of his reign – and with good reason. Between his inability to stem the rising tide of debt and his recurrent rows with the House of Commons, James left his son a difficult inheritance. He did even more lasting damage to his dynasty. Many of his subjects interpreted his willingness to exchange a religious toleration for the infanta as a sign that he was soft on Catholicism, and the Overbury affair only confirmed their worst fears about his seriously defective moral compass.

Yet while these were serious issues – and ones that would bedevil his successor – they should not obscure his achievements.

First and foremost, he survived, and that was no mean achievement in itself. In Scotland, between the aristocratic rivalries and the religious turmoil, James seemed destined either to be the Kirk's puppet or to be deposed, just as his mother had been. Ironically, notwithstanding the long odds there, he eventually triumphed, and shrewdly exploiting periodic advantages, he came to dominate both the Kirk and his nobles. He was less fortunate in England, where even the considerable energies of the first King of Great Britain could not make much headway against profound xenophobia and serious financial problems. In the end, he probably did about as well as any foreign monarch could have done with English Parliament-men. But the stalemate with the Commons helps explain his near-complete devotion to country life. Perhaps his son, who was rapidly becoming anglicized, would have more luck in Westminster. In the meantime, he might as well enjoy the countryside with a few close friends. Nevertheless, in spite of this failing, he had a profound impact on the nation.

He used his authority to give England something that it had not seen in a generation – two decades of peace during which trade boomed and the country prospered. His devotion to peace extended into his administrative style. Notwithstanding his rhetoric about the divine right of kings, he was more interested in articulating than in implementing it. While he exploited Bate's case to collect impositions, this victory did not lead to other major revenue experiments, certainly nothing on the scale of the ship money levies that his son collected in the 1630s. As a result, his wealthier subjects may well have grumbled about his policies, but not about their tax burden, which was remarkably light during his reign. Admittedly his decision to keep Britain out of the spiralling continental conflict in the early 1620s was controversial, agitating many in the Commons and in his family. Perhaps he was being too cautious. Yet given the disasters that befell Charles I in the late 1620s when he led Britain to war, James probably was being realistic about his inability to project power in central Europe. Quite simply, he thought he could do little militarily to assist Elizabeth and Frederick.

His protracted struggle against Scottish Presbyterians had made him deeply appreciative of the more moderate Elizabethan Church. While his four English predecessors had each overhauled the Church, he did not. Instead he retained the basic ecclesiastical structure he inherited from his cousin, and by resisting calls from the godly for further reformation, he allowed his English subjects to become comfortable with a certain style of worship. While he periodically recalibrated his theological position to gain political leverage, he remained at heart a moderate Calvinist, and his faith is still visible today in the translation of the Bible he authorized.

His greatest public achievement, however, was Great Britain, which for him was the eminently logical outcome because 'God first united these two kingdoms, both in language, religion, and similitude of manners'. To those

Englishmen opposed to union, he argued with characteristic wit: 'what God has conjoined then, let no man separate.'[1]

He was deeply stung by the Westminster Parliament's stubborn resistance to an Anglo-Scottish Union, and the pain was still evident in 1621 when he lamented to the new session: 'I have often piped unto you, and you have not danced.' Nevertheless he continued to drag both states towards a union. In 1604, he insisted on being addressed as the King of Great Britain, and in 1606 he ordered both English and Scottish vessels to fly 'the Red Cross, commonly called St George's Cross, and the White Cross, commonly called St Andrew's Cross, joined together according to a form made by our Heralds'.[2] The fact that his creations – Great Britain and the Union Flag – are still very much in evidence serves as a striking visual reminder of King James's importance.

These public achievements should not obscure his private one. Effectively orphaned as an infant, taught to despise his mother, regularly beset by violence, and hobbled by a disability, he might well have become hopelessly neurotic. Yet he found peace in the countryside even though his discovery eventually cost thousands of animals their lives. In that tranquil setting, he established himself as a leading public intellectual, and he created the family he had never had with his hunting crew. In his last hours at Theobalds with his childhood friend the Earl of Kellie beside him, he may have recalled Lady Minny, George Buchanan, Grandfather Lennox, the Ruthven raiders and Kellie's older brother, who died defending James.

Compared to those upsetting times, he had certainly found earthly paradise at Theobalds, surrounded by his son and a few close friends, many books, large deer herds and packs of dogs, facing his end in the arms of the person he loved best.

In 1584, James had published his poem about the phoenix to honour his Franco-Scottish friend the Duke of Lennox. But shortly after James's death, an anonymous author extended the metaphor to include James himself by praising 'The Phoenix poems of a Phoenix king'.[3] It seems at first an unusual description of James VI and I, but as we crane our necks to examine the ceiling at the Banqueting House, it seems an eminently appropriate one for a monarch flying upwards.

Notes

ABBREVIATIONS

Bellany	Alastair Bellany, *The Politics of Court Scandal in Early Modern England: News Culture and the Overbury Affair, 1603–1660* (Cambridge: Cambridge University Press, 2002)
Bergeron	*King James and Letters of Homoerotic Desire*, ed. David Bergeron (Iowa City: University of Iowa Press, 1999)
Calderwood	David Calderwood, *The Historie of the Kirk of Scotland*, ed. Thomas Thomson, 8 vols (Edinburgh: Wodrow Society, 1842–9)
CD 1621	*Commons Debates 1621*, ed. Wallace Notestein et al. (New Haven, Conn.: Yale University Press, 1935)
Colville	John Colville, *Original Letters of Mr. John Colville, 1582–1603*, ed. D. Laing (Edinburgh: Bannatyne Club, 1858)
Correspondence	*The Correspondence of Elizabeth Stuart, Queen of Bohemia*, ed. Nadine Akkerman, 2 vols (Oxford: Oxford University Press, 2011 and 2015)
CSPS	*Calendar of State Papers, Scotland*, ed. J. Bain et al., 11 vols (London: HMSO, 1891–1936)
CSPV	*Calendar of State Papers ... Venice*, ed. H. Brown and Allen B. Hinds, vols 10–18 (London: HMSO, 1900–1911)
ESL	*Early Stuart Libels*, ed. Alastair Bellany and Andrew McRae, www.earlystuartlibels.net
Fuller	Thomas Fuller, *Church History of Great Britain*, 3 vols (London: William Tegg, 1868)
Goodman	Godfrey Goodman, *The Court of King James the First*, ed. John S. Brewer, 2 vols (London: Richard Bentley, 1839)
Guy	John Guy, *My Heart is My Own: The Life of Mary Queen of Scots* (London: Harper Perennial, 2004)
Harington	Sir John Harington, *Nugae Antiquae: Being a Miscellaneous Collection ... During the Reigns of Henry VIII, Edward VI, Queen Mary, Elizabeth, and King James*, 2 vols (London: Vernon and Hood, 1804)
HMC Mar	*Historical Manuscripts Commission: Supplementary Report on the Manuscripts of the Earl of Mar*, ed. H. Paton (London: HMSO, 1930)
Letters	*Letters of King James VI and I*, ed. G. P. V. Akrigg (Berkeley, Calif.: University of California Press, 1984)
Murder	Alastair Bellany and Thomas Cogswell, *The Murder of King James I* (New Haven, Conn.: Yale University Press, 2015)

ODNB	*Oxford Dictionary of National Biography* online edition
'Phaeton's Chariot'	Thomas Cogswell, 'Phaeton's Chariot: The Parliament-men and the Continental Crisis in 1621', in *The Political World of Thomas Wentworth, Earl of Strafford 1621–1641*, ed. Julia Merritt (Cambridge: Cambridge University Press, 1996), pp. 24–46
Poems	*The Poems of King James I of Scotland*, ed. James Craigie, 2 vols (Edinburgh: Scottish Text Society, 1955 and 1958)
Political Writings	*King James VI and I: Political Writings*, ed. J. P. Sommerville (Cambridge: Cambridge University Press, 1994)
PP 1626	*Proceedings in Parliament 1626*, ed. William Bidwell and Maija Jansson (New Haven, Conn.: Yale University Press, 1991)
Proclamations	*Stuart Royal Proclamations: The Royal Proclamations of King James I*, ed. Paul Hughes and James Larkin (Oxford: Oxford University Press, 1973)
Regales	*Regales Aphorismi or a Royal Chain of Golden Sentences ... Delivered by King James* (London: 1650)
Russell	Conrad Russell, *King James VI and I and His English Parliaments*, ed. R. Cust and A. Thrush (Oxford: Oxford University Press, 2011)
Scott	*The Secret History of the Court of James the First*, ed. Walter Scott, 2 vols (Edinburgh: 1811)
TNA SP	The National Archives, State Papers: 14 and 15 (Domestic: James I) and 52 (Scotland Series I: Elizabeth I)
Workes	James I, *The Workes of the Most High and Mightie Prince, Iames* (London: 1616)

PROLOGUE: ABOVE ALL THE SPORTSMEN IN THE WORLD

1. TNA SP 15/42/41; and *CSPV*, XV, p. 259. For a fuller version of this sketch of James late in life, see *Murder*, pp. 1–24. See also Alan Stewart's important essay 'Government by Beagle: The Impersonal Government of James VI and I', in *Renaissance Beasts: Of Animals, Humans and Other Wonderful Creatures*, ed. Erica Fudge (Urbana, Ill.: University of Illinois Press, 2004), pp. 101–15.

2. *CSPV*, XVII, p. 411.

3. Scott, I, p. 364, n. z; *CSPV*, X, p. 454; and *The Oglander Memoirs*, ed. W. H. Long (London: Reeves and Turner, 1888), pp. 132–4.

4. *CSPV*, X, p. 70, and XII, p. 41; *CSPS*, VII, p. 275; and TNA SP 14/143/22.

5. Harington, I, pp. 351–2; and Goodman, I, pp. 173–4.

6. *CSPV*, XVI, p. 412.

7. Harington, I, pp. 351–2; Calderwood, III, p. 393; and *The Letters of Sir Robert Moray*, ed. D. Stevenson (Aldershot: Ashgate, 2007).

8. *ESL*, L5 and nn. 7, 10 and 11.

9. Sir Anthony Weldon, *The Court and Character of King James* (London: 1651), reprinted in Scott, I, p. 360. See also Michael Young, *King James VI and I and the History of Homosexuality* (London: Palgrave Macmillan, 2000); David Bergeron,

Royal Family, Royal Lovers: King James of Scotland and England (Columbia: University of Missouri Press, 1991); and Alan Bray, *Homosexuality in Renaissance England* (London: Gay Men's Press, 1982).

1. A BOY WITH A SPARROWHAWK

1. Guy, pp. 219–370.
2. *Letters*, p. 41. See also Maurice Lee, Jr, *James Stewart, Earl of Moray: A Political Study of the Reformation in Scotland* (New York: Columbia University Press, 1953); and Amy Blakeway, *Regency in Sixteenth-Century Scotland* (Woodbridge: Boydell & Brewer, 2015).
3. *The Autobiography and Diary of James Melville* (Edinburgh: Wodrow Society, 1842), p. 48. See also Roger Mason, 'George Buchanan, James VI and the Presbyterians', in his *Scots and Britons: Scottish Political Thought and the Union of 1603* (Cambridge: Cambridge University Press, 1994), pp. 112–38.
4. George Buchanan, *A Detection* (London: 1689), p. 72; George MacKenzie, *Lives and Characters of the . . . Scots Nation*, 3 vols (Edinburgh: 1711–22), III, p. 180; and *Murder*, pp. 105–9.
5. *CSPS*, V, pp. 287 and 318.
6. *Letters*, p. 98.
7. Calderwood, III, p. 642, and IV, p. 406; and *The Border Papers: Calendar of the Letters and Papers Relating to the Borders of England and Scotland*, ed. J. Bain, 2 vols (Edinburgh: HM General Register House, 1894 and 1896), I, p. 83.
8. *The Register of the Privy Council of Scotland*, ed. P. Hume Brown, vol. 3 (Edinburgh: HM General Register House, 1901), p. 595.
9. Calderwood, III, p. 649; Caroline Bingham, *The Making of a King: The Early Years of James VI and I* (London: Collins, 1968), pp. 175–6; and *The Historie of King James the Sext*, ed. T. Thomason (Edinburgh: J. Ballantyne, 1825), p. 191.
10. *CSPS*, VI, pp. 561 and 564.
11. *Records of the Parliaments of Scotland* (www.rsp.ac.uk) 1585/5/14.

2. THE HAT WITH THE JEWELLED 'A'

1. *CSPS*, VII, p. 274.
2. On Maitland, see Maurice Lee, Jr, *John Maitland of Thirlestane and the Foundation of the Stewart Despotism in Scotland* (Princeton, NJ: Princeton University Press, 1959).
3. *CSPS*, VII, pp. 338 and 363.
4. *Letters*, p. 78; and Calderwood, IV, p. 606. See also Guy, pp. 396–502.
5. Colville, p. 316; and *CSPS*, IX, p. 650.
6. TNA SP 52/38, f. 101; Calderwood, V, pp. 169 and 171; *New Poems of James I of England*, ed. A. Westcott (New York: Columbia University Press, 1911), p. 44; Colville, p. 316; and *CSPS*, VII, p. 274, and IX, p. 701.

7. David Stevenson, *Scotland's Last Royal Wedding: The Marriage of James VI and Anne of Denmark* (Edinburgh: John Donald, 1997).

8. *Poems*, II, pp. 82 and 90–92. See also Ian Campbell and Aonghus MacKechnie, 'The "Great Temple of Solomon" at Stirling Castle', *Architectural History*, 54 (January 2011), pp. 91–118.

9. *Letters*, p. 137; and *CSPS*, IX, p. 704, and X, p. 11.

10. James VI, *Daemonologie* (Edinburgh: 1597), sig. A2.

11. *CSPS*, X, p. 11.

12. Calderwood, V, p. 440. See also *Andrew Melville (1545–1622): Writings, Reception and Reputation*, ed. R. Mason and S. Reid (Farnham: Ashgate, 2014).

13. Calderwood, IV, pp. 351, 487 and 583, and V, pp. 161, 304 and 378.

14. Calderwood, IV, pp. 675, 698, 710. See also IV, pp. 488, 500 and 711.

15. *Political Writings*, pp. 5–6, 25–6 and 63–4.

16. W. F. Arbuckle, 'The Gowrie Conspiracy', *Scottish Historical Review*, 36 (1957), pp. 1–24 and 89–110.

17. *Letters of Queen Elizabeth and King James VI of Scotland*, ed. J. Bruce, Camden Old Series 46 (London: Camden Society, 1849), pp. 85, 109, 115, 122, 164 and 169; and *Letters*, p. 173. See also Susan Doron, 'Loving and Affectionate Cousins? The Relationship between Elizabeth I and James VI, 1586–1603', in *Tudor England and Its Neighbours*, ed. S. Doron and G. Richardson (Basingstoke: Palgrave Macmillan, 2005), pp. 203–34.

3. THE MIRROR OF GREAT BRITAIN

1. *Political Writings*, p. 166.

2. *The Progresses ... of James the First*, ed. John Nichols, 4 vols (London: J. B. Nichols, 1828), I, p. 140. For more details of his journey, see pp. 1–144.

3. Lawrence Stone, *The Crisis of the Aristocracy: 1558–1641* (Oxford: Oxford University Press, 1965), p. 24.

4. Keith Brown, 'Monarchy and the Government of Britain', in *Short Oxford History of the British Isles: The Seventeenth Century*, ed. J. Wormald (Oxford: Oxford University Press, 2008), pp. 13–48; and Diana Newton, *The Making of the Jacobean Regime: James VI and I and the Government of England, 1603–1605* (Woodbridge: Boydell Press, 2005).

5. *Letters*, pp. 269 and 261; and *Regales*, p. 112.

6. *Letters*, p. 280; Harington, I, pp. 351–2; and Goodman, I, pp.173–4.

7. *ESL*, E5 and E6.

8. *Letters*, p. 250.

9. *Gradus Simeonis* (London: 1649), TT E.55/17, p. 6. On Herbert, see Edward, Earl of Clarendon, *The History of the Rebellion* (London: William Cole, 1826), I, p. 105; and Neil Cuddy, 'The Revival of the Entourage: The Bedchamber of James I, 1603–25', in *The English Court: From the Wars of the Roses to the Civil War*, ed. D. Starkey (London: Longman, 1987), pp. 173–225.

10. *Letters*, pp. 278–9 and 233.

11. *Letters*, p. 255; and *CSPV*, X, pp. 70, 195, 469 and 510.

12. *Minor Prose Works of King James VI and I*, ed. James Craigie (Edinburgh: Scottish Text Society, 1982), p. 99; and J. A. Sharpe, *The Bewitching of Anne Gunter* (London: Profile Books, 1999), pp. 169–97.

13. Russell, pp. 14–42.
14. *Letters*, p. 255.
15. *Regales*, pp. 10–11.
16. Fuller, III, p. 210.
17. *Cobbett's Complete Collection of State Trials*, vol. 2 (London: R. Bagshaw, 1809), p. 229. See also Mark Nicholls, *Investigating Gunpowder Plot* (Manchester: Manchester University Press, 1991).
18. *Political Writings*, p. 152.

4. PARLIAMENT ROBES

1. *Letters*, p. 291. On Salisbury, Pauline Croft, 'Robert Cecil, Earl of Salisbury', *ODNB*.
2. K. Fincham and P. Lake, 'The Ecclesiastical Policy of James I', *Journal of British Studies*, 24 (1985), pp. 169–209.
3. *Political Writings*, p. 200. See also Michael Questier, 'The Politics of Religious Conformity and the Accession of James I', *Historical Research*, 71 (1998), pp. 14–30.
4. Fuller, II, p. 711.
5. *Political Writings*, pp. 86 and 92. See also Michael Questier, 'Catholic Loyalism in Early Stuart England', *English Historical Review*, 123 (2008), pp. 1132–65.
6. *Workes*, sig. d2.
7. *The Holy Bible* (London: 1612), sig. A2.
8. *The Oxford History of the British Empire*, vol. 1: *The Origins of Empire: British Overseas Enterprise to the Close of the Seventeenth Century*, ed. Nicholas Canny (Oxford: Oxford University Press, 2001), pp. 1–240.
9. Pauline Croft, 'Fresh Light on Bate's Case', *Historical Journal*, 30 (1987), pp. 923–35.
10. *Political Writings*, pp. 202–3. See also Russell, pp. 74–94.
11. *Letters*, pp. 316–17; G. Chapman, B. Jonson and J. Marston, *Eastward Hoe* (1605), III.iii.42–5; and *ESL*, E5 and E7.
12. *Letters*, pp. 317–18; and *CSPV*, III, p. 102.
13. *Letters*, p. 318. See also Eric Lindquist, 'The Failure of the Great Contract', *Journal of Modern History*, 57 (1985), pp. 617–51.

5. BROCADES AND LACE

1. Harington, I, p. 375. See also Alastair Bellany, 'Robert Carr, Earl of Somerset', *ODNB*.
2. *CSPV*, XII, p. 41, and XV, p. 388.
3. Noel Malcolm, *De Dominis, 1560–1624: Venetian, Anglican, Ecumenist and Relapsed Heretic* (London: Strickland & Scott, 1984); and *Murder*, pp. 92–114.
4. James I, *Declaration Concerning ... the Cause of D. Conradus Vorstius* (London: 1612), p. 6.

5. *Corona Regia*, ed. W. Schleiner (Geneva: Droz, 2010), pp. 81 and 89.
6. Markku Peltonen, *The Duel in Early Modern England* (Cambridge: Cambridge University Press, 2006), pp. 1–145; and Malcolm Smuts, 'The Making of *Rex Pacificus*: James VI and I and the Problem of Peace in an Age of Religious War', in *Royal Subjects: Essays on the Writings of James VI and I*, ed. D. Fischlin and M. Fortier (Detroit: Wayne State University Press, 2002), pp. 371–87.
7. *CSPV*, XV, p. 392.
8. Laura Stewart, 'The Political Repercussions of the Five Articles of Perth: A Re-assessment of James VI and I's Religious Policies in Scotland', *Sixteenth Century Journal*, 38 (2007), pp. 1013–36.
9. *Workes*, sig. [d] and e-e2v.
10. Samuel Clarke, *The Lives of Thirty-two English Divines* (London: 1677), p. 81. See also George Ruggle, *Ignoramus* (London: 1615).
11. *Proceedings in Parliament 1614* (Philadelphia: American Philosophical Society, 1988), pp. xxii, 142–4 and 423. See also Russell, pp. 95–122.
12. Pauline Croft, 'The Catholic Gentry, the Earl of Salisbury and the Baronets of 1611', in *Conformity and Orthodoxy in the English Church, 1560–1660*, ed. P. Lake and M. Questier (Woodbridge: Boydell Press, 2000), pp. 262–81; and Paul Sellin, *Treasure, Treason and the Tower: El Dorado and the Murder of Sir Walter Raleigh* (Farnham: Ashgate, 2011), pp. 217–62.
13. *Letters*, p. 362. See also Frederick Dietz, *English Public Finance, 1558–1641* (London: Century, 1932), pp. 144–81.
14. *CSPV*, XII, pp. 448 and 472.
15. Bodleian Library, MS Wood, 30, 32, fo. 107r, quoted in Bellany, p. 236.
16. *Letters*, pp. 336–9 and 343. On this involved affair, see Bellany.
17. *Letters*, p. 316; and Bellany, p. 244.
18. *Political Writings*, p. 209.
19. *The Petition . . . of the Poore Commons* (London: 1642), p. 5.

6. GORGET AND ARMOUR

1. *Political Writings*, p. 134.
2. *CSPV*, XVI, p. 456; and XVII, pp. 410, 441 and 583; and *HMC Mar*, II, p. 153.
3. Bergeron, pp. 149 and 188. See also Roger Lockyer, *Buckingham: The Life and Political Career of George Villiers, First Duke of Buckingham, 1592–1628* (Harlow: Longman, 1981).
4. Bergeron, pp. 148–9 and 180; and *Political Writings*, p. 230.
5. *Poems*, II, p. 175.
6. *Correspondence*, I, pp. 114 and 193.
7. *Correspondence*, I, p. 279; and *CD 1621*, II, p. 10. See also Brennan Pursell, *The Winter King: Frederick V of the Palatinate and the Coming of the Thirty Years War* (Aldershot: Ashgate, 2003), pp. 11–166.
8. *CSPV*, XVI, p. 150. See also David Hebb, *Piracy and the English Government* (Aldershot: Scolar Press, 1994).
9. *CSPV*, XVI, pp. 363 and 496.
10. *Proclamations*, p. 394; and *CD 1621*, II, pp. 2 and 10. See also 'Phaeton's Chariot', p. 35.
11. 'Phaeton's Chariot', p. 30.

12. *CD 1621*, II, p. 2; and *Political Writings*, pp. 256–7 and 262. See also Brennan Pursell, 'Gondomar and the Dissolution of the Parliament of 1621', *History*, 85 (2000), pp. 428–45.
13. *Poems*, II, pp. 180–81. See also Thomas Cogswell, 'England and the Spanish Match', in *Conflict in Early Stuart England*, ed. Richard Cust and Ann Hughes (Harlow: Longman, 1989), pp. 107–33.
14. Bergeron, p. 150; and *Letters*, p. 394.
15. *Letters*, pp. 395, 397 and 408.
16. *Poems*, II, pp. 190 and 193.
17. *Letters*, pp. 400–401, 411 and 415–16. See also Glyn Redworth, *The Prince and the Infanta: The Cultural Politics of the Spanish Match* (New Haven, Conn.: Yale University Press, 2004).

7. AN OLD MAN AND A NEW MARRIAGE

1. *HMC Mar*, II, pp. 181–3.
2. *The Journal of the House of Commons*, vol. 3 (London: HMSO, 1802), pp. 208–10.
3. Bergeron, p. 201. See also Thomas Cogswell, *The Blessed Revolution: English Politics and the Coming of War, 1621–1624* (Cambridge: Cambridge University Press, 1989).
4. *Cabala, Mysteries of State, in Letters of the Great Ministers of K. James and K. Charles* (London: 1653), p. 276. See also Robert Ruigh, *The Parliament of 1624* (Cambridge, Mass.: Harvard University Press, 1971), pp. 257–302.
5. Bergeron, p. 203; and *Murder*, pp. 22–3.
6. *Letters*, p. 438.
7. Bergeron, pp. 174–5.
8. *Murder*, pp. 68–91.
9. George Eglisham, *The Forerunner of Revenge* (Frankfort [Brussels]: 1626), p. 21; and *Proceedings in Parliament, 1626*, ed. William Bidwell and Maija Jansson, 4 vols (New Haven, Conn.: Yale University Press, 1991–2), I, p. 480.
10. *Mercurius Elencticus*, no. 19 (5 April 1648), pp. 143–5. See also *Murder*, pp. 429–30.

CONCLUSION: THE PHOENIX KING

1. *Political Writings*, p. 135.
2. *CD 1621*, II, p. 2; and *Proclamations*, p. 135.
3. Additional manuscript poems in the Lambeth Palace Library's edition of James's 1584 *Essayes*. See also Sebastian Verweij, ' "Booke, go thy ways": The Publication, Reading, and Reception of James VI/I's Early Poetic Works', *Huntington Library Quarterly*, 77 (2014), pp. 111–31.

Further Reading

Anyone trying to understand James VI and I should begin by examining his remarkable output of poetry and prose, and in this task it is useful to begin with Jane Rickard, *Authorship and Authority: The Writings of James VI and I* (Manchester: Manchester University Press, 2002). Fortunately there are several excellent modern editions, and chief among them are: *The Letters of King James VI and I*, edited by G. P. V. Akrigg (Berkeley, Calif.: University of California Press, 1984); *King James VI and I: Political Writings*, edited by Johann Sommerville (Cambridge: Cambridge University Press, 1994); and *The Poems of James VI of Scotland*, edited by James Craigie, 2 vols (Edinburgh: Scottish Text Society, 1955 and 1958). His personal letters to Somerset and Buckingham are particularly revealing, and pending the publication of a careful edition of these with contemporary spellings and an analysis of their provenance, there is much to applaud in *King James and Letters of Homoerotic Desire*, edited by David Bergeron (Iowa City: University of Iowa Press, 1999).

Given D. H. Willson's palpable dislike of James, a sentiment that runs through his *King James VI and I* (New York: Henry Holt, 1956), we badly need a new, full-scale biography of the man. Until then, Willson's book should be read together with Alan Stewart's perceptive *The Cradle King: A Life of James VI and I* (London: Chatto & Windus, 2003). Those readers in more of a hurry will enjoy Pauline Croft, *King James I* (London: Palgrave Macmillan, 2002), and Roger Lockyer, *James VI and I* (Harlow: Longman, 1998). Of the many older biographies, few can surpass the insights in Caroline Bingham, *The Making of a King: The Early Years of James VI and I* (London: Collins, 1968).

Jenny Wormald began the James's scholarly re-evaluation with 'James VI and I: Two Kings or One?', *History*, 67 (1983), pp. 187–209, and Alan Stewart presented a new appreciation of him in 'Government by Beagle: The Impersonal Government of James VI and I', in *Renaissance Beasts: Of Animals, Humans and Other Wonderful Creatures*, edited by Erica Fudge (Urbana, Ill.: University of Illinois Press, 2004), pp. 101–15. James's sexuality has attracted much recent attention; among the new works, see Michael Young, *King James VI and I and the History of Homosexuality* (London: Palgrave Macmillan, 2000), and David Bergeron, *Royal Family, Royal Lovers: King James of Scotland and England* (Columbia: University of Missouri Press, 1991).

On his Scottish reign, see Aysha Pollnitz, 'Education and Royal Resistance: George Buchanan and James VI and I', in *Princely Education in Early Modern England* (Cambridge: Cambridge University Press, 2015), pp. 264–313; Julian Goodare, *The Government of Scotland, 1560–1625* (Oxford: Oxford University Press, 2004), and *State and Society in Early Modern Scotland* (Oxford: Clarendon Press, 1999); Keith Brown, *Bloodfeud in Scotland, 1573–1625* (Edinburgh: John Donald, 1986); Christina Larner, *Enemies of God: The Witch Hunt in Scotland* (London: Chatto & Windus, 1981); Roger Mason, *Scots and Britons: Scottish Political Thought and the Union of 1603* (Cambridge: Cambridge University Press, 1994); and Maurice Lee, Jr, *John Maitland of Thirlestane and the Foundation of the Stewart Despotism in Scotland* (Princeton, NJ: Princeton University Press, 1959), and *Government by Pen: Scotland Under James VI and I* (Urbana, Ill.: University of Illinois Press, 1980). For primary sources, the *Calendar of State Papers, Scotland*, edited by J. Bain et al., 11 vols (London: HMSO, 1891–1936), is particularly comprehensive. Nothing, however, can surpass the excellence of David Calderwood's remarkable – and delightful – *The Historie of the Kirk of Scotland*, edited by Thomas Thomson, 8 vols (Edinburgh: Wodrow Society, 1842–9).

For his time in England, an abundance of information on James's personal and public life can be found in *The Progresses . . . of James the First*, edited by John Nichols, 4 vols (London: J. B. Nichols, 1828); and the *Calendar of State Papers ... Venice*, edited by H. Brown and Allen B. Hinds, vols 10–18 (London: HMSO, 1900–1911). We must anxiously await editions of the exceptionally vivid correspondence in the Trumbull MSS, held at the British Library, but in the meantime we can still enjoy *The Letters of John Chamberlain*, edited by Norman McClure (Philadelphia: American Philosophical Society, 1939).

His early years in England have attracted erratic scholarly attention. The Scotsmen who accompanied James to Whitehall desperately need further study, but their importance can be clearly seen in Neil Cuddy's influential essay 'The Revival of the Entourage: The Bedchamber of James I, 1603–25', in *The English Court: From the Wars of the Roses to the Civil War*, edited by D. Starkey (London: Longman, 1987), pp. 173–225. Likewise further work needs to be done on James's financial problems, and the best place to begin this vital task is Frederick Dietz, *English Public Finance, 1558–1641* (London: Century, 1932); and John Cramsie, *Kingship and Crown Finance Under King James VI and I, 1603–1625* (London: Boydell & Brewer, 2002). On James's troubled early relations with the House of Commons, see Linda Levy Peck, *Northampton: Patronage and Policy at the Court of James I* (London: Allen & Unwin, 1982); and Conrad Russell, *King James VI and I and His English Parliaments*, edited by R. Cust and A. Thrush (Oxford: Oxford University Press, 2011).

The end of his reign has had better scholarly coverage. On the steadily worsening continental crisis and the trip to Madrid, see Glyn Redworth, *The Prince and the Infanta: The Cultural Politics of the Spanish Match* (New Haven, Conn.: Yale University Press, 2003). On James's latter parliamentary sessions, see Robert Zaller, *The Parliament of 1621: A Study in Constitutional Conflict* (Berkeley, Calif.: University of California Press, 1971); Thomas Cogswell, *The Blessed Revolution: Politics and the Coming of War, 1621–1624* (Cambridge: Cambridge University Press, 1989); and Conrad Russell, *Parliaments and English Politics, 1621–1629* (Oxford: Clarendon

Press, 1979), pp. 1–203. Although James himself is poorly understood for this period, a favourite and a chief minister has been well studied: see Roger Lockyer, *Buckingham: The Life and Political Career of George Villiers, First Duke of Buckingham, 1592–1628* (Harlow: Longman, 1981); and Menna Prestwich, *Cranfield: Politics and Profits Under the Early Stuarts: The Career of Lionel Cranfield, Earl of Middlesex* (Oxford: Clarendon Press, 1966).

Given James's extensive theological training, religion played a main role in Jacobean England. Novices should begin with an excellent overview of his ecclesiastical policies, Kenneth Fincham and Peter Lake, 'The Ecclesiastical Policy of King James I', *Journal of British Studies*, 24 (1985), pp. 169–209, and they should then proceed to Patrick Collinson, *The Religion of Protestants: The Church in English Society, 1559–1625* (Oxford: Clarendon Press, 1982); Kenneth Fincham, *Pastor as Prelate: The Episcopate of James I* (Oxford: Clarendon Press, 1990); Nicholas Tyacke, *Anti-Calvinists: The Rise of English Arminianism, c.1590–1640* (Oxford: Clarendon Press, 1987); and W. B. Patterson, *King James I and the Reunion of Christendom* (Cambridge: Cambridge University Press, 2000).

On the scandals of his reign, see David Coast, *News and Rumour in Jacobean England, 1618–1625* (Manchester: Manchester University Press, 2014); Alastair Bellany, *The Politics of Court Scandal in Early Modern England: News Culture and the Overbury Affair, 1603–1660* (Cambridge: Cambridge University Press, 2002); and Alastair Bellany and Thomas Cogswell, *The Murder of King James I* (New Haven, Conn.: Yale University Press, 2015).

Picture Credits

1. Portrait of James VI and I as a child, late sixteenth century, by an unknown artist (© National Portrait Gallery, London)
2. Adrian Vanson (attr.), portrait of James VI and I, 1595 (Scottish National Portrait Gallery)
3. John de Critz, portrait of James VI and I, 1604 (Scottish National Portrait Gallery)
4. Portrait of James VI and I in his state clothes, 1610, by an unknown artist (Guildhall Feoffment Trust/St Edmundsbury Heritage Service)
5. Portrait of James VI and I, c.1615, by an unknown artist (The Old Schools, University of Cambridge)
6. Paul van Somer, portrait of James VI and I, 1618 (Royal Collection Trust/© Her Majesty Queen Elizabeth II, 2016)
7. Adam de Colone (circle of), portrait of James VI and I, 1623 (National Trust for Scotland, Culzean Castle, Garden & Country Park)
8. Sir Peter Paul Rubens, ceiling of the Banqueting House, London, 1636 (© Tate, London, 2015)

Acknowledgements

I am grateful to Simon Winder for asking me to write this volume and then for gently nudging me to finish it. On the editorial side, Anna Hervé effortlessly sorted out several thorny issues, and Kate Parker admirably succeeded in the unenviable task of smoothing out my unruly prose.

It was my extraordinary good fortune to have written it while at the Huntington Library in San Marino, California, amid its exemplary collection of English and Scottish materials. For their good humour while I repeatedly pestered them, I am much obliged to the Research Director, Steve Hindle; to his staff, Juan Gómez and Carolyn Powell; and to my neighbours in the Upper Munger, Dena Goodman, Amanda Herbert, Daniel Immerwahr, Adam Mosley, and Carol and François Rigolot. High praise is due to Norm Jones, who provided me with Elizabethan comparisons and much advice, and to Will Cavert who, over coffee at the library, supplied a wonderful reference to James's obsession with dogs. Every morning as I badgered them for entrance as early as possible, the guards, especially Lou Ann Bonanza, James Michère, Marco Pérez and Patricia Vanley, daily taught me that it is possible to be dutiful *and* kind.

Finally, this book owes a great deal to many conversations with Alastair Bellany and to our recent work, *The*

ACKNOWLEDGEMENTS

Murder of King James I. Richard Cust, Ken Fincham, James Knowles, Peter Lake, Roger Mason and Michael Questier gave me invaluable assistance with early drafts – and Georgia Warnke with life.

The book is dedicated in memory of my brother, who would have enjoyed reading about King James.

Index

Penguin Monarchs

THE HOUSES OF WESSEX AND DENMARK

Athelstan*	Tom Holland
Aethelred the Unready	Richard Abels
Cnut	Ryan Lavelle
Edward the Confessor	David Woodman

THE HOUSES OF NORMANDY, BLOIS AND ANJOU

William I*	Marc Morris
William II*	John Gillingham
Henry I	Edmund King
Stephen*	Carl Watkins
Henry II*	Richard Barber
Richard I*	Thomas Asbridge
John	Nicholas Vincent

THE HOUSE OF PLANTAGENET

Henry III*	Stephen Church
Edward I*	Andy King
Edward II*	Christopher Given-Wilson
Edward III*	Jonathan Sumption
Richard II*	Laura Ashe

THE HOUSES OF LANCASTER AND YORK

Henry IV	Catherine Nall
Henry V*	Anne Curry
Henry VI*	James Ross
Edward IV*	A. J. Pollard
Edward V	Thomas Penn
Richard III	Rosemary Horrox

* Now in paperback

THE HOUSE OF TUDOR

Henry VII	Sean Cunningham
Henry VIII*	John Guy
Edward VI*	Stephen Alford
Mary I*	John Edwards
Elizabeth I*	Helen Castor

THE HOUSE OF STUART

James I*	Thomas Cogswell
Charles I*	Mark Kishlansky
[Cromwell*	David Horspool]
Charles II*	Clare Jackson
James II*	David Womersley
William III & Mary II*	Jonathan Keates
Anne	Richard Hewlings

THE HOUSE OF HANOVER

George I*	Tim Blanning
George II	Norman Davies
George III	Amanda Foreman
George IV	Stella Tillyard
William IV*	Roger Knight
Victoria*	Jane Ridley

THE HOUSES OF SAXE-COBURG & GOTHA AND WINDSOR

Edward VII*	Richard Davenport-Hines
George V*	David Cannadine
Edward VIII*	Piers Brendon
George VI*	Philip Ziegler
Elizabeth II*	Douglas Hurd

* Now in paperback

ALLEN LANE
an imprint of
PENGUIN BOOKS

Also Published

David Wallace-Wells, *The Uninhabitable Earth: A Story of the Future*

Randolph M. Nesse, *Good Reasons for Bad Feelings: Insights from the Frontier of Evolutionary Psychiatry*

Anand Giridharadas, *Winners Take All: The Elite Charade of Changing the World*

Richard Bassett, *Last Days in Old Europe: Triste '79, Vienna '85, Prague '89*

Paul Davies, *The Demon in the Machine: How Hidden Webs of Information Are Finally Solving the Mystery of Life*

Toby Green, *A Fistful of Shells: West Africa from the Rise of the Slave Trade to the Age of Revolution*

Paul Dolan, *Happy Ever After: Escaping the Myth of The Perfect Life*

Sunil Amrith, *Unruly Waters: How Mountain Rivers and Monsoons Have Shaped South Asia's History*

Christopher Harding, *Japan Story: In Search of a Nation, 1850 to the Present*

Timothy Day, *I Saw Eternity the Other Night: King's College, Cambridge, and an English Singing Style*

Richard Abels, *Aethelred the Unready: The Failed King*

Eric Kaufmann, *Whiteshift: Populism, Immigration and the Future of White Majorities*

Alan Greenspan and Adrian Wooldridge, *Capitalism in America: A History*

Philip Hensher, *The Penguin Book of the Contemporary British Short Story*

Paul Collier, *The Future of Capitalism: Facing the New Anxieties*

Andrew Roberts, *Churchill: Walking With Destiny*

Tim Flannery, *Europe: A Natural History*

T. M. Devine, *The Scottish Clearances: A History of the Dispossessed, 1600-1900*

Robert Plomin, *Blueprint: How DNA Makes Us Who We Are*

Michael Lewis, *The Fifth Risk: Undoing Democracy*

Diarmaid MacCulloch, *Thomas Cromwell: A Life*

Ramachandra Guha, *Gandhi: 1914-1948*

Slavoj Žižek, *Like a Thief in Broad Daylight: Power in the Era of Post-Humanity*

Neil MacGregor, *Living with the Gods: On Beliefs and Peoples*

Peter Biskind, *The Sky is Falling: How Vampires, Zombies, Androids and Superheroes Made America Great for Extremism*

Robert Skidelsky, *Money and Government: A Challenge to Mainstream Economics*

Helen Parr, *Our Boys: The Story of a Paratrooper*

David Gilmour, *The British in India: Three Centuries of Ambition and Experience*

Jonathan Haidt and Greg Lukianoff, *The Coddling of the American Mind: How Good Intentions and Bad Ideas are Setting up a Generation for Failure*

Ian Kershaw, *Roller-Coaster: Europe, 1950-2017*

Adam Tooze, *Crashed: How a Decade of Financial Crises Changed the World*

Edmund King, *Henry I: The Father of His People*

Lilia M. Schwarcz and Heloisa M. Starling, *Brazil: A Biography*

Jesse Norman, *Adam Smith: What He Thought, and Why it Matters*

Philip Augur, *The Bank that Lived a Little: Barclays in the Age of the Very Free Market*

Christopher Andrew, *The Secret World: A History of Intelligence*

David Edgerton, *The Rise and Fall of the British Nation: A Twentieth-Century History*

Julian Jackson, *A Certain Idea of France: The Life of Charles de Gaulle*

Owen Hatherley, *Trans-Europe Express*

Richard Wilkinson and Kate Pickett, *The Inner Level: How More Equal Societies Reduce Stress, Restore Sanity and Improve Everyone's Wellbeing*

Paul Kildea, *Chopin's Piano: A Journey Through Romanticism*

Seymour M. Hersh, *Reporter: A Memoir*

Michael Pollan, *How to Change Your Mind: The New Science of Psychedelics*

David Christian, *Origin Story: A Big History of Everything*

Judea Pearl and Dana Mackenzie, *The Book of Why: The New Science of Cause and Effect*

David Graeber, *Bullshit Jobs: A Theory*

Serhii Plokhy, *Chernobyl: History of a Tragedy*

Michael McFaul, *From Cold War to Hot Peace: The Inside Story of Russia and America*

Paul Broks, *The Darker the Night, the Brighter the Stars: A Neuropsychologist's Odyssey*

Lawrence Wright, *God Save Texas: A Journey into the Future of America*

John Gray, *Seven Types of Atheism*

Carlo Rovelli, *The Order of Time*

Mariana Mazzucato, *The Value of Everything: Making and Taking in the Global Economy*

Richard Vinen, *The Long '68: Radical Protest and Its Enemies*

Kishore Mahbubani, *Has the West Lost It?: A Provocation*

John Lewis Gaddis, *On Grand Strategy*

Richard Overy, *The Birth of the RAF, 1918: The World's First Air Force*

Francis Pryor, *Paths to the Past: Encounters with Britain's Hidden Landscapes*

Helen Castor, *Elizabeth I: A Study in Insecurity*

Ken Robinson and Lou Aronica, *You, Your Child and School*

Leonard Mlodinow, *Elastic: Flexible Thinking in a Constantly Changing World*

Nick Chater, *The Mind is Flat: The Illusion of Mental Depth and The Improvised Mind*

Michio Kaku, *The Future of Humanity: Terraforming Mars, Interstellar Travel, Immortality, and Our Destiny Beyond*

Thomas Asbridge, *Richard I: The Crusader King*

Richard Sennett, *Building and Dwelling: Ethics for the City*

Nassim Nicholas Taleb, *Skin in the Game: Hidden Asymmetries in Daily Life*

Steven Pinker, *Enlightenment Now: The Case for Reason, Science, Humanism and Progress*

Steve Coll, *Directorate S: The C.I.A. and America's Secret Wars in Afghanistan, 2001 - 2006*

Jordan B. Peterson, *12 Rules for Life: An Antidote to Chaos*

Bruno Maçães, *The Dawn of Eurasia: On the Trail of the New World Order*

Brock Bastian, *The Other Side of Happiness: Embracing a More Fearless Approach to Living*

Ryan Lavelle, *Cnut: The North Sea King*

Tim Blanning, *George I: The Lucky King*

Thomas Cogswell, *James I: The Phoenix King*

Pete Souza, *Obama, An Intimate Portrait: The Historic Presidency in Photographs*

Robert Dallek, *Franklin D. Roosevelt: A Political Life*

Norman Davies, *Beneath Another Sky: A Global Journey into History*

Ian Black, *Enemies and Neighbours: Arabs and Jews in Palestine and Israel, 1917-2017*

Martin Goodman, *A History of Judaism*

Shami Chakrabarti, *Of Women: In the 21st Century*

Stephen Kotkin, *Stalin, Vol. II: Waiting for Hitler, 1928-1941*

Lindsey Fitzharris, *The Butchering Art: Joseph Lister's Quest to Transform the Grisly World of Victorian Medicine*

Serhii Plokhy, *Lost Kingdom: A History of Russian Nationalism from Ivan the Great to Vladimir Putin*

Mark Mazower, *What You Did Not Tell: A Russian Past and the Journey Home*

Lawrence Freedman, *The Future of War: A History*

Niall Ferguson, *The Square and the Tower: Networks, Hierarchies and the Struggle for Global Power*

Matthew Walker, *Why We Sleep: The New Science of Sleep and Dreams*

Edward O. Wilson, *The Origins of Creativity*

John Bradshaw, *The Animals Among Us: The New Science of Anthropology*

David Cannadine, *Victorious Century: The United Kingdom, 1800-1906*

Leonard Susskind and Art Friedman, *Special Relativity and Classical Field Theory*

Maria Alyokhina, *Riot Days*

Oona A. Hathaway and Scott J. Shapiro, *The Internationalists: And Their Plan to Outlaw War*

Chris Renwick, *Bread for All: The Origins of the Welfare State*

Anne Applebaum, *Red Famine: Stalin's War on Ukraine*

Richard McGregor, *Asia's Reckoning: The Struggle for Global Dominance*

Chris Kraus, *After Kathy Acker: A Biography*

Clair Wills, *Lovers and Strangers: An Immigrant History of Post-War Britain*

Odd Arne Westad, *The Cold War: A World History*

Max Tegmark, *Life 3.0: Being Human in the Age of Artificial Intelligence*

Jonathan Losos, *Improbable Destinies: How Predictable is Evolution?*

Chris D. Thomas, *Inheritors of the Earth: How Nature Is Thriving in an Age of Extinction*

Chris Patten, *First Confession: A Sort of Memoir*

James Delbourgo, *Collecting the World: The Life and Curiosity of Hans Sloane*

Naomi Klein, *No Is Not Enough: Defeating the New Shock Politics*

Ulrich Raulff, *Farewell to the Horse: The Final Century of Our Relationship*

Slavoj Žižek, *The Courage of Hopelessness: Chronicles of a Year of Acting Dangerously*

Patricia Lockwood, *Priestdaddy: A Memoir*

Ian Johnson, *The Souls of China: The Return of Religion After Mao*

Stephen Alford, *London's Triumph: Merchant Adventurers and the Tudor City*

Hugo Mercier and Dan Sperber, *The Enigma of Reason: A New Theory of Human Understanding*

Stuart Hall, *Familiar Stranger: A Life Between Two Islands*

Allen Ginsberg, *The Best Minds of My Generation: A Literary History of the Beats*

Sayeeda Warsi, *The Enemy Within: A Tale of Muslim Britain*

Alexander Betts and Paul Collier, *Refuge: Transforming a Broken Refugee System*

Robert Bickers, *Out of China: How the Chinese Ended the Era of Western Domination*

Erica Benner, *Be Like the Fox: Machiavelli's Lifelong Quest for Freedom*

William D. Cohan, *Why Wall Street Matters*

David Horspool, *Oliver Cromwell: The Protector*

Daniel C. Dennett, *From Bacteria to Bach and Back: The Evolution of Minds*

Derek Thompson, *Hit Makers: How Things Become Popular*

Harriet Harman, *A Woman's Work*

Wendell Berry, *The World-Ending Fire: The Essential Wendell Berry*

Daniel Levin, *Nothing but a Circus: Misadventures among the Powerful*

Stephen Church, *Henry III: A Simple and God-Fearing King*

Pankaj Mishra, *Age of Anger: A History of the Present*

Graeme Wood, *The Way of the Strangers: Encounters with the Islamic State*

Michael Lewis, *The Undoing Project: A Friendship that Changed the World*

John Romer, *A History of Ancient Egypt, Volume 2: From the Great Pyramid to the Fall of the Middle Kingdom*

Andy King, *Edward I: A New King Arthur?*

Thomas L. Friedman, *Thank You for Being Late: An Optimist's Guide to Thriving in the Age of Accelerations*

John Edwards, *Mary I: The Daughter of Time*

Grayson Perry, *The Descent of Man*

Deyan Sudjic, *The Language of Cities*

Norman Ohler, *Blitzed: Drugs in Nazi Germany*

Carlo Rovelli, *Reality Is Not What It Seems: The Journey to Quantum Gravity*

Catherine Merridale, *Lenin on the Train*

Susan Greenfield, *A Day in the Life of the Brain: The Neuroscience of Consciousness from Dawn Till Dusk*

Christopher Given-Wilson, *Edward II: The Terrors of Kingship*

Emma Jane Kirby, *The Optician of Lampedusa*

Minoo Dinshaw, *Outlandish Knight: The Byzantine Life of Steven Runciman*

Candice Millard, *Hero of the Empire: The Making of Winston Churchill*

Christopher de Hamel, *Meetings with Remarkable Manuscripts*

Brian Cox and Jeff Forshaw, *Universal: A Guide to the Cosmos*

Ryan Avent, *The Wealth of Humans: Work and Its Absence in the Twenty-first Century*

Jodie Archer and Matthew L. Jockers, *The Bestseller Code*

Cathy O'Neil, *Weapons of Math Destruction: How Big Data Increases Inequality and Threatens Democracy*

Peter Wadhams, *A Farewell to Ice: A Report from the Arctic*

Richard J. Evans, *The Pursuit of Power: Europe, 1815-1914*

Anthony Gottlieb, *The Dream of Enlightenment: The Rise of Modern Philosophy*

Marc Morris, *William I: England's Conqueror*

Gareth Stedman Jones, *Karl Marx: Greatness and Illusion*

J.C.H. King, *Blood and Land: The Story of Native North America*

Robert Gerwarth, *The Vanquished: Why the First World War Failed to End, 1917-1923*

Joseph Stiglitz, *The Euro: And Its Threat to Europe*

John Bradshaw and Sarah Ellis, *The Trainable Cat: How to Make Life Happier for You and Your Cat*

A J Pollard, *Edward IV: The Summer King*

Erri de Luca, *The Day Before Happiness*

Diarmaid MacCulloch, *All Things Made New: Writings on the Reformation*

Daniel Beer, *The House of the Dead: Siberian Exile Under the Tsars*

Tom Holland, *Athelstan: The Making of England*

Christopher Goscha, *The Penguin History of Modern Vietnam*

Mark Singer, *Trump and Me*

Roger Scruton, *The Ring of Truth: The Wisdom of Wagner's Ring of the Nibelung*

Ruchir Sharma, *The Rise and Fall of Nations: Ten Rules of Change in the Post-Crisis World*

Jonathan Sumption, *Edward III: A Heroic Failure*

Daniel Todman, *Britain's War: Into Battle, 1937-1941*

Dacher Keltner, *The Power Paradox: How We Gain and Lose Influence*

Tom Gash, *Criminal: The Truth About Why People Do Bad Things*

Brendan Simms, *Britain's Europe: A Thousand Years of Conflict and Cooperation*

Slavoj Žižek, *Against the Double Blackmail: Refugees, Terror, and Other Troubles with the Neighbours*

Lynsey Hanley, *Respectable: The Experience of Class*

Piers Brendon, *Edward VIII: The Uncrowned King*

Matthew Desmond, *Evicted: Poverty and Profit in the American City*

T.M. Devine, *Independence or Union: Scotland's Past and Scotland's Present*